I0701238

Crime Trivia Large Print

1,001 Fun Facts and Anecdotes Related to the Fascinating and Dark Underworld of Crime Trivia

Crime Trivia Large Print

1,001 Fun Facts and Anecdotes Related to the Fascinating and Dark Underworld of Crime Trivia

Copyright 2024

Adicus Abbott

The facts and trivia questions in this text are presented for entertainment purposes only. They are correct to the best of the author's knowledge. This is the large print edition of *Crime Trivia*.

ISBN: 9798332150111

Independently Published

Welcome true crime trivia fans.

Enjoy the facts, stats, and anecdotes.

And please, stay behind the yellow crime scene tape.

Adicus Abbott

Table of Contents

The Fascinating World of Crime

The infamous bank robber and jewel thief, Willie Sutton, was once asked, "Why do you rob banks?" According to an article in *The Saturday Evening Post* from January 1951, Willie smirked and replied, "Because that's where the money is."

Years later, Willie Sutton denied ever saying that, and claimed the journalist conducting the interview exaggerated an old adage common among thieves, which simply stated, "go where the money is."

In the world of crime, that opens a lot of doors, from bank robbery, to second story home burglary, to online phishing and email scams, to car warranty telemarketers, fake IRS audit claims, and even Wall Street insider trading.

Technically, the Willie Sutton quote is correct. Banks do have money. But would you want it?

The quickest way to invite the Federal Bureau of Investigation (FBI) into your life is to commit a federal crime. Kidnapping and bank robbing top the list, and virtually guarantee an instantaneous federal response, with the further consequences of federal, big house, incarceration.

In fact, according to FBI crime statistics, the average bank robber makes off with $7,500. No doubt leaving the bank premises with traceable serial numbers and a variety pack of ink bombs, as well as a crime punishable by up to 20 years in federal incarceration. Due to the violence associated with bank robbery, whether a fire arm was used or not, prison sentences are tough, with very few early releases.

Around 20% of bank robberies are solved, which may sound like a low percentage, but thieves don't just commit one robbery and hang up their proverbial outlaw spurs. No, they gain confidence with each heist, and become habitual offenders. How many banks could a guy rob before ending up like John Wojtowicz, whose unsuccessful attempt to rob a bank led to the 1975 movie, *Dog Day Afternoon*? Maybe four, if you're lucky.

Rather than robbing banks, a guy may do well to roam the streets and alleys of his hometown, collecting empty beer cans and discarded water bottles. Imagine the lawyer fees and headaches avoided with simple, honest labor in exchange for a little dough?

But courts, jails, and lawyer waiting rooms are not filled with people who measure risk and reward on the same scale as law abiding citizens. They want a shortcut to the so-called "Life of Reilly," and accept the associated risks as tolerable costs of doing business…evident in the George Washington letter sent to Thomas Jefferson in 1786. According to Washington, "Paper money has had the effect in your state that it will ever have, to ruin commerce, oppress the honest, and open the door to every species of fraud and injustice."

Echoing Washington and Jefferson's low opinion of a fiat, paper, currency, an early 20th century economist named Milton Friedman once stated, "Only government can take perfectly good paper, cover it with perfectly good ink and make the combination worthless."

Worthless or not, criminals consider the pursuit of ill-gotten gain a worthwhile endeavor.

Fast Facts

1. On 13 February 1866, associates of Jesse James and Frank James robbed a bank in Liberty, Missouri. It was the first recorded bank robbery in U.S. history. Amazingly, they netted over $60,000 in the heist.
2. J.L Hunter Rountree has the dubious honor of being the oldest known bank robber in America. His last heist netted $1,999. He was 92 at the time.
3. Most bank robberies in the U.S. occur on Fridays.
4. During the COVID pandemic, cyber attacks on banks rose by 238%.
5. Bonnie Parker and Clyde Barrow managed to evade capture for a couple years as they robbed banks during the 1930s. The infamous couple was ambushed and killed by local police and

Texas Ranger Frank Hamer, on 23 May 1934 in Louisiana. They were shot 167 times.

The criminal mind simply can't resist the allure of "easy" money.

To put crime in more contemporary terms, the FBI Crime in the United States Report paints a bleak picture for our cities. For example, Washington D.C. saw significant increases in crime from 2022 to 2023. Specifically:

- Motor Vehicle Theft Up 86%
- Homicides Up 36%
- Robberies Up 68%
- Violent Crimes Up 39%
- Burglaries Up 4%
- Total Crime Up 26%

Nationwide, the murder rate has jumped 46% over the past two years, rape is up 12%, and aggravated assault is up 22%.

Clearly, something is rotten in Denmark. Some crime experts blame the rise in crime on inflation and systemic social injustices, while others point a finger at lax enforcement of laws, cashless bail policies, drug addiction, a nationwide mental health crisis, and homelessness.

Whatever side of this argument you choose to accept as gospel, crime is real, and it's not going anywhere. Which is why *Crime Trivia* exists.

When you're ready, turn the page and start reading, or select a topic of interest to you from the Table of Contents, or simply open this book to any page for a random taste of crime trivia, fun facts, and anecdotes.

Public Enemy Era Gangsters

Comedian Jeff Foxworthy does a routine where he jokes about how women think they want a "dangerous" man…until he does something dangerous.

At the core of this joke is a simple truth, dangerous men (and women) are like live action train wrecks. They're unforgettable, and capture some primal, evil back alley corner of our imaginations.

Discover a handful of dangerous men and women from the 1920s and 1930s…a time in America known as the Public Enemy Era.

Bonnie and Clyde

Nearly one hundred years after the deaths of Bonnie Parker and Clyde Barrow, their two year bank robbery and killing spree continues to capture the attention of true crime buffs.

Bonnie and Clyde were both born into poverty near Dallas, Texas. Clyde was from West Dallas, and Bonnie was from a neighboring down near Dallas known as Cement City. Over the course of their crime spree, Bonnie and Clyde killed 12 police officers and civilians. They died on 23 May 1934 in an ambush staged by Texas Ranger, Frank Hamer, along with police officers from Dallas and Louisiana, and Frank's Texas Ranger partner, Maney Gault.

While the exact numbers vary, it is estimated that Bonnie and Clyde were shot 167 times. The Bonnie and Clyde "Death Car" is on display and free to see at Whiskey Pete's Casino in Primm, Nevada. Sitting next to it is a shot up car owned by Al Capone.

- Clyde Barrow was born on 24 March 1909 in Tellico, Texas, southeast of Dallas.

- Bonnie Parker was born on 1 October 1910 in Rowena, Texas, southwest of Dallas.

- Clyde grew up in a suburb of Dallas, known as West Dallas. He was the son of a cotton sharecropper.

- Bonnie grew up in a suburb of Dallas known as Cement City. Raised by a single mother, following the death of her father when she was four years old.

- Bonnie was married to a petty thug and thief named Roy Thornton before she met Clyde. She wore a wedding ring and was never technically divorced from Roy.

- Texas Ranger Frank Hamer was reputed to have killed 53 men in over 100 separate gunfights during his career. He was shot 17 times, and survived.

- Frank Hamer was technically retired from the Texas Rangers when he was recalled to active duty to hunt down Bonnie and Clyde.

Al Capone

Al Capone, also known as Scarface, rose to notoriety in Chicago during the Prohibition days between 1920 and 1933.

Prohibition was an act of Congress that outlawed the production, importation, transportation, and sale of alcoholic beverages. But of course, people's appetite for alcohol didn't just disappear because Congress made a law. In fact, some of the most violent times in true crime history took place during the years of Prohibition, revolving around the black market smuggling and sell of alcohol to a thirsty public.

At the top of the bootlegging and mob control of alcohol production, distribution, and sale, were urban gangs, typically of Irish and Italian descent. And at the top of the gang pile was a ruthless man named Al Capone, head of an Italian crime organization known as the Outfit.

Capone was convicted of tax evasion and sentenced to prison in May 1932. He served his time in both Atlanta and Alcatraz Federal Penitentiaries until his release in November 1939. Despite his history of violence and his commanding role of the Outfit, Capone did not fare well in prison. He was often tormented and harassed by other inmates, and was even stabbed, and superficially wounded by a fellow inmate, in 1936.

- Capone left school for good when he was 14 after punching a teacher in the face.

- While Capone came from Brooklyn, he gained his notoriety in Chicago.

- While working as a bouncer on Coney Island, Capone reportedly insulted a young woman. The woman's brother slashed his face with a knife, giving Capone his nickname, Scarface.

- Capone moved to Chicago in 1919 to join a gang he had run with in New York.

- Capone was 26 years old when he assumed control of the Outfit gang in 1924.

- Capone's Outfit gang netted around $100 million per year during the 1920s, from clubs, bootlegging, gambling, and prostitution.

- Al Capone's brother James Capone, was a Prohibition agent in Nebraska.

Al Capone died at his home in Florida of a stroke, followed by heart failure, on 25 January 1947.

George "Baby Face" Nelson

Baby Face Nelson will go down in Depression era gangsters and bank robbers history as the one who killed more FBI agents than any other street thug of his time.

Lester Joseph Gillis, also known as George Nelson, and Baby Face Nelson, was born in Chicago in 1908.

He died 27 November 1934 in a shootout with the FBI. Nelson took two FBI agents with him, Agents Herman Hollis and Samuel Cowley. Leading up to his death, Nelson had led a string of bank robberies and wild shootouts, partnered with John Dillinger, and had earned a top spot of the FBI's Most Wanted list. At the time of his death, Nelson was ranked Public Enemy No. 1.

- At the age of 12, Nelson shot a playmate in the jaw with a gun he had found. Nelson spent a year in the state reformatory for his first major offense.
- On 6 January 1930, Nelson and a group of his associates barged into the home of a magazine executive named Charles M. Richter. They managed to loot the house for over $205,000 worth of jewelry.

- Nelson robbed his first bank on 21 April, 1930. He netted $4,000 from the heist.

- Nelson and his gang attempted to rob a roadhouse on 23 November 1930. They left three dead, following a brief gunfight.

- Nelson allegedly committed his first murder on 26 November 1930 when he shot and killed a stockbroker named Edwin Thompson during a robbery.

- Nelson was arrested in late 1931, and was looking at life in prison. He escaped during a prison transfer in February 1932 and fled west to Reno, Nevada, and later, California.

- By August 1933, Nelson was back in the Midwest and took up the trade of bank robbing in earnest.

- John Dillinger used a wooden pistol to escape from jail on 3 March 1934, presumably with the assistance of Nelson.

- Baby Face Nelson John Dillinger, and Pretty Boy Floyd were identified as the robbers of the Merchants National Bank in South Bend, Indiana on 30 June 1934.

- John Dillinger was ambushed and killed by FBI agents in Chicago on 22 July 1934, followed by the death of Pretty Boy Floyd on 22 October 1934. Their deaths elevated Baby Face Nelson to Public Enemy No. 1.

John Dillinger

John Herbert Dillinger was a notorious bank robber and gangster who operated in the Chicago and St Louis areas during the turbulent 1930s. The FBI ranked him as Public Enemy No. 1.

Following various daring bank robberies and prison escapes, Dillinger hid out in Chicago in July 1934, using the alias Jimmy Lawrence, a petty criminal from Wisconsin who Dillinger resembled. Dillinger believed he was anonymous in a large city. What he didn't realize was that Chicago was ground zero for the FBI dragnet tasked with hunting him down.

Unlike Bonnie and Clyde, who preferred the back roads and camping in the woods, Dillinger loved the bright city lights. His love for clubbing, hanging around beautiful women, and frequenting the theater, led to his demise. Dillinger died in an FBI ambush, led by the famous G-Man, Melvin Purvis, on 22 July 1934 outside the Biograph Theater in Chicago.

- The last movie John Dillinger saw was the *Manhattan Melodrama*. Released in 1934 and starring Clark Gable, the movie holds a Rotten Tomato Audience Score of 71%.

- Dillinger is implicated in 12 separate bank robberies, between 21 June 1933, and 30 June 30 1934.

- Souvenir hunters dipped newspapers and handkerchiefs into the pool of blood beneath the dead Dillinger.

- Dillinger's body was put on public display in the Cook County Morgue. 15,000 dropped by to have a look, and four death masks were made.

- Dillinger is buried at the Crown Hill Cemetery in Indianapolis. His headstone has been replaced four times due to souvenir hunters chipping off pieces of the stone.

- One of the Dillinger death masks is on public display at the Alcatraz East museum in Pigeon Forge, Tennessee. The mark of the exit wound from a bullet is clearly visible beneath Dillinger's right eye.

Pretty Boy Floyd

Charles Arthur Floyd, known as Pretty Boy Floyd, was a bank robber who operated in the central part of the United States, especially Oklahoma. Although Floyd was a bank robber and suspected murderer, he was well liked by the common people who believed he burned mortgage documents during his robberies.

Following the death of John Dillinger in July 1934, J. Edgar Hoover promoted Floyd to Public Enemy No. 1. Floyd died by gunshot wounds sustained in an FBI ambush in East Liverpool, Ohio led by FBI agent Melvin Purvis on 22 October 1934.

- Floyd's last words, according to FBI agents involved in his ambush shooting, were, "I'm done for. You've hit me twice."
- Floyd made $120 in his last bank robbery.
- At his death, Floyd had a watch with 10 notches on it, reportedly indicating the number of people he had killed.
- Floyd's funeral in Akins, Oklahoma reportedly drew 40,000 people, the largest funeral in Oklahoma history.
- Floyd was arrested for a payroll robbery on 16 September 1925, in St. Louis, Missouri and served three years in prison before being paroled.
- Floyd earned the nickname "Pretty Boy" because of the nice clothes he wore while working on oil rigs.

Lesser Known Gangsters of the Time

The 1930s were a turbulent and violent time in America. Due to sensational news reporting, the Great Depression, nationwide manhunts from the newly formed Federal Bureau of Investigation under J. Edgar Hoover, and the public's fascination with bank robbers, people like Pretty Boy Floyd, John Dillinger, and Baby Face Nelson gained celebrity status. Here are a few of the other gun running gangsters from the Public Enemy Era.

Kate Barker, known as **Ma Barker**, was the matriarch of the Barker-Karpis Gang. J. Edgar Hoover once described Ma Barker as "the most vicious, dangerous, and resourceful criminal brain of the last decade." Ma Barker died in a shootout with FBI agents in 1935 in Ocklawaha, Florida. The Barker family crime spree spanned the years 1910 to 1939. On 13 January 1939, Arthur Barker, one of Ma's sons, died in an escape attempt from Alcatraz Federal Penitentiary.

George Kelly Barnes, known as **Machine Gun Kelly**, died from a heart attack in the Leavenworth Federal Penitentiary in 1954 following his 1933 conviction of kidnapping Oklahoma oil magnate Charles Urschel on 22 July 1933. Kelly earned his nickname due to his frequent use of a Thompson submachine gun in his criminal activities. He is also reputed to be the source of the phrase "G-Men" to describe FBI agents, like Melvin Purvis.

Benjamin Siegel, known as **Bugsy Siegel**, was a bootlegger who turned to gambling following the repeal of Prohibition. Bugsy is well known as one of the key mob figures behind the rise of Las Vegas, and a possible hitman for various Jewish and Italian mobs. Bugsy was shot dead by a sniper in Beverly Hills on 20 June 1947. His killer has never been identified.

Charles "Lucky" Luciano is reportedly the founder of the modern American crime family movement, known as the National Crime Syndicate. In 1936 Lucky was convicted of running a prostitution ring, but was later released and deported to Italy to provide Naval intelligence during the Second World War. Unlike many of his mob colleagues, Lucky died on 26 January 1962, rather than at the hands of an FBI ambush.

Arthur Flegenheimer, known as **Dutch Schultz**, ran with New York City's infamous Five Families crime syndicate (Bonanno, Colombo, Gambino, Genovese, and Lucchese), and was known for extortion and running numbers games (an early form of the Pick 3 Lottery), as well as killing, when necessary. Dutch died on 24 October 1935 from an infection caused by a gunshot wound. He was apparently shot by a member of his own crime family because he attempted to kill the famous New York prosecutor Thomas Dewey, in direct violation of the Godfather's order not to bother the prosecutor.

John "Red" Hamilton was a Canadian gangster and bank robber who often ran with John Dillinger. He died from a gunshot wound sustained during an armed robbery on 26 April 1934. Red was also known as Three Finger Jack, due to a childhood sledding accident that chopped off two if his fingers on his right hand. Red gained notoriety on 26 September 1933 when he escaped with nine other members of the John Dillinger gang from the Indiana State Prison, including Harry "Pete" Pierpont.

Harry "Pete" Pierpont ran with John Dillinger and Red Hamilton, and was a convicted bank robber and murderer. Pierpont was executed in the electric chair in Ohio on 17 October 1934. Harry spent several of his childhood years in the state reformatory. One reform school superintendent described Harry as "wild as a March Hare." Pierpont's final act of defiance came on 22 September 1934 when he attempted to escape Death Row. Pierpont was shot multiple times in the escape attempt, and was still suffering from gunshot wounds when he was carried by gurney to the electric chair for execution.

Vincent "Mad Dog" Coll was a mob assassin and kidnapper. He is notorious for his brutality, and was even implicated in the accidental death of a child in the course of a kidnapping. But accident or not, when a person is killed in the process of committing a crime, it's murder. Coll got his start as an armed guard for beer trucks under Dutch Schultz. His effectiveness led Dutch to hire him as an assassin, where he excelled. By 1930, Coll and Dutch were rival gang leaders and enemies. On 8 February 1932, Coll was ambushed and shot to death while using a phone booth. His killers were never identified.

The Long Arm of the Law

There was a time in America when local police and sheriff's departments broke off a police chase at the county or state line. For the thugs, gangsters, and bank robbers of the Public Enemy Era, that all changed when their bootlegging, racketeering, and bank robbing grabbed the attention of the feds, and the Bureau of Investigation, later known as the Federal Bureau of Investigation, deployed G-Men like Melvin Purvis to hunt down the culprits and end their life of crime.

- On 26 July 1908, the U.S. Attorney General Charles Bonaparte created the Bureau of Investigation. It did not become known as the FBI until 1935.
- The original purpose of the FBI was to audit and investigate financial transactions in the federal courts. Agents were accountants.
- J. Edgar Hoover became the head of the FBI in 1924 and remained at that post until his death in 1972. He had served 48 years with the FBI, and essentially created the investigative procedures we know to this day.
- The FBI considered the movie, *It's A Wonderful Life*, communist propaganda due to its portrayal of the banking industry.
- The FBI created its Top Ten Most Wanted list in 1950. Since then, it has captured 465 out of 494 criminals on its list.
- Hoover was not enthusiastic about women serving as agents. The first female agents started after his death in 1972.
- The FBI waited until 2012 to digitize its crime files.

- The FBI considers hair samples found at crime scenes to be one of its best clues to the identity of a criminal. It keeps over 5,000 hair samples for use in comparison for determining a criminal's ethnicity.

The Rise of Video Surveillance

In terms of being watched, tracked, or identified, Clyde Barrow, John Dillinger, and even Al Capone, had it easy compared to today's gangsters, thugs, bank robbers, and would be public enemies.

Thanks to the ubiquitous presence of surveillance cameras, facial recognition software, GPS tracking, and modern forensic analysis of crime scenes, crime sprees are mostly abbreviated.

Surveillance cameras are particularly hazardous to a criminal's career and include: traffic cameras, toll booth cameras, live webcams in public spaces, surveillance cameras from banks, retail stores, ATM machines, and residential home security systems. And lately, the addition of civilian dash cams in cars, as well as body and dash cameras on police officers.

- According to statistics collected by IHS Markit, China leads the world in its use of surveillance cameras with over 626 million cameras in use. That equates to 439 cameras per 1,000 people.

- Outside of China, the 10 most video surveilled cities in the world, by population, include: Hyderabad, Indore, Delhi, Singapore, Moscow, Baghdad, Seoul, St. Petersburg, London, and Los Angeles.

- In terms of cameras per square mile, the top 10 surveilled cities in the world include: Delhi, Seoul, Singapore, Hyderabad, New York, Moscow, London, Chennai, Mumbai, and Dhaka.

- There are currently over 1 billion government owned and controlled surveillance cameras in use around the world. This number does not include privately owned security cameras.

Despite the heavy prevalence of surveillance cameras in major cities around the world, IHS Markit found little correlation between the number of employed cameras and crime rates. However, while cameras may do little to dissuade criminals, they are effective in the apprehension of criminals and documentation of their crimes in court proceedings.

Another common use of surveillance cameras is the growing popularity of home security systems and door cameras. Across the nation over 400 police departments have pooled their resources with various neighborhood watch type organizations to expand their surveillance of communities. While it sounds draconian, many of these programs have assisted in the safe return of missing persons, especially children.

In one case in Bakersfield, California, an at-risk teenage girl had wandered away from home, apparently lost. Police conducted a reverse 911 call to residents of her neighborhood, and within minutes 12 different residents reported seeing the missing teen on their home security cameras. Minutes later the police located the teen and helped her return home safely.

Gruesome Serial Killers

The ultimate crime against humanity is the forceful taking of another human's life. The killers discussed below have found their way into the history books by being the best (or worse, depending upon your perspective) at what they do.

According to statistics maintained by the University of Michigan, there have been 3,600 serial killers in American history. This summary of cases discussed below includes a handful of American serial killers, as well as a few of the more notorious cases from around the world.

John Wayne Gacy

One of the most notorious and spooky serial killers in American history was a man named John Wayne Gacy.

Gacy tortured and raped his male victims, and is believed to have killed 33 young men, whom he mostly buried in the crawlspace beneath his house. He was active between 1972 and 1978, and lived in Norwood Park Township, near Chicago, Illinois. His preferred method of killing was strangulation.

Gacy was executed by lethal injection on 10 May 1994. His last known words were addressed to a prison guard, who claims Gacy said, "kiss my ass."

Herman H. H. Holmes Mudgett

Herman Webster Mudgett, better known as H.H. Holmes, was an American con artist and serial killer active between 1891 and 1894. He is best remembered for his murderous acts during the Chicago World's Columbian Exposition (World's Fair) in 1893.

Holmes confessed to killing 27 people, but was actually only convicted for the death of his business partner, Benjamin Pitezel.

Some criminal experts believe Holmes' killing did not technically measure up to "serial killer" status, as the documented murders he committed were generally carried out as a means of quieting his business partner and other associates in order to protect his con artist schemes. At the time of the murders, Holmes was accused by the press of killing as many as 200 people in a hotel he built, called the "Murder Castle," in anticipation of the crowds who would be visiting Chicago to celebrate the World's Fair.

Whether Holmes only killed one person or 200 remains a mystery. What's not a mystery is that the state executed Holmes by hanging on 7 May 1896.

Gary Ridgway

Gary Ridgway, also known as the Green River Killer, is considered one of the most prolific serial killers in American history, killing at least 49 people, and possibly up to 71, between the years 1982 to 1998.

Ridgway operated in the Seattle area, while living in Renton, Washington. Ridgway chose vulnerable women, such as prostitutes and runaways as his victims. His preferred method of killing the women was strangulation. He earned the name "Green River Killer" from the river near where he most frequently dumped the bodies.

Ridgway was arrested on 30 November 2001. He confessed to the murders in a plea bargain to avoid the death penalty. He is currently serving life in prison, without parole, in Walla Walla, Washington.

Jeffrey Dahmer

Tracey Edwards may be one of the luckiest men alive. On 22 July 1991, Edwards met up with notorious serial killer and reputed cannibal, Jeffrey Dahmer.

Dahmer talked Edwards into going home with him to presumably pose for nude photographs and watch the movie *The Exorcist* together. Once at Dahmer's home, Dahmer handcuffed him and threatened to cut his heart out. Edwards somehow managed to escape the home and was picked up by police wandering the streets with a set of handcuffs dangling from one wrist.

Edwards guided police back to the Dahmer residence, where the police found extensive photographic evidence of Dahmer's brutality, as well as multiple human body parts, including severed heads, in his refrigerator.

Jeffrey Dahmer was active in the Milwaukee area from 1978 to 1991. He is connected to 17 murders, primarily of gay black men. He was killed in prison by a fellow inmate on 28 November 1994.

In a nationwide survey, Jeffrey Dahmer ranked second among those polled for the serial killer they would like to be pen pals with. Ted Bundy took the top slot. Other infamous killers to top the list included: Jack the Ripper, Aileen Wuornos, Charles Manson, Dennis Rader, and Gary Ridgway.

Marcel Dr. Satan Petiot

Marcel Petiot, also known as Dr. Satan, was a psychotic killer from Paris, France during the Second World War.

Using the panic and confusion of the war as cover, Petiot created a fake escape network and convinced people fleeing the Nazis to pay him for passage out of France. Once the escapees met Petiot at his home, they were advised they required inoculation before beginning the arduous journey out of occupied France. Of course, the only vaccination he administered was a dose of cyanide poisoning. After death, Petiot would cremate his victims in a basement coal stove and bury the remains in the basement.

Eventually, a neighbor noticed the smell of a burning body and informed the police. During the investigation, police recovered 40 suitcases in his home, suggesting he claimed at least 40 lives in his reign of terror. They also recovered pieces of 63 different people in his basement graveyard.

Petiot evaded capture for seven months, using the alias, Henri Valeri. When he was finally recognized and arrested, Petiot was carrying a pistol, 31,700 francs, and 50 sets of identity documents. Petiot was beheaded on 25 May 1946, following a three day delay due to a malfunctioning guillotine.

Edmund Kemper

Edmund Kemper, also known as the Co-ed Killer, was active in the Santa Cruz, California area from May 1972 to April 1973. During this time he killed 10 people, including his mother and her best friend, as well as female college students he picked up as hitchhikers around Santa Cruz. Years earlier, he had killed his paternal grandparents at the age of 15.

Most of his murders included necrophilia, decapitation, and dismemberment. Kemper requested the death penalty, but was sentenced to 8 consecutive life sentences. He is currently incarcerated in California. Police and prison guards call him "Big Ed" due to his height. Kemper stands 6'9" tall.

Dennis Lynn Rader

Dennis Rader, also known as the BTK killer for Blind, Torture, Kill, was a serial killer in the Wichita, Kansas area between 1974 to 1991.

Rader was notorious for sending taunting letters to the police that detailed his killings. In 2005 he was arrested and pled guilty. He is currently serving multiple life sentences in a Kansas prison. Rader preferred female targets, and used strangulation or suffocation with a plastic bag to kill his victims.

During his killing spree, Rader claimed at least 10 lives and is considered a sexual sadist. He is college educated, with a degree in Administrative Justice.

Some interesting fast facts regarding the BTK killer include:

- Rader was a church council president and Cub Scout leader.
- Rader murdered an entire family of four in 1974.
- Rader named himself the BTK Killer.
- Rader installed home security systems for a living, some of which were installed because of fears of the BTK Killer.
- Officials used Rader's daughter's DNA to catch him.
- Rader had already picked out his next victim when he was arrested.

Felonious Stupidity

With the possible exception of serial killers who use their wits to extend their killing sprees over years, most criminals are not the sharpest tacks in the drawer.

For example, in 2015, John Mogan and Ashley Duboe decided to rob a bank. Elated with their bravado and seeming success, they shared pictures of themselves with the money on Facebook. Hours later they were arrested.

In yet another example of criminal stupidity, in March of 2010 two men decided to rob a bank by calling ahead. One of the men called the bank and told a teller to get $100,000 ready for pick up. At the same time the call was made, an accomplice to the bank robber was in the bank, presumably ready to pick up the bag of cash.

Sadly for the bank robbers, the teller alerted police and the bank was surrounded. The subsequent discovery and arrest of the bank robber inside the bank led to the arrest of his colleague.

But our hapless "call ahead" bank robbers are not alone in their misguided attempts to live on the lamb. In fact, if stupidity were a crime, these criminal masterminds would be doing life without parole.

On 26 March 2008 a young man attempted to rob a muffler shop in Chicago. He presented a gun and demanded an employee open the shop safe. The employee told the robber only the owner could open the safe.

Frustrated, the robber left two phone numbers with the muffler shop employee and told him to call him when the owner returned to the shop. After the robber left, the employee called the police. When police arrived they called the numbers. Sure enough, the robber took the bait and returned to the muffler shop armed and ready to rob the safe.

But even then, the robber did not go peacefully, but chose to engage in a gunfight with police. The robber was arrested after sustaining a non life threatening bullet wound.

****

Blake Leak was fleet of foot, but rather short in the thinking department. While trying to burglarize a New York convenience store he was confronted by two police officers.

Putting his running abilities to work, he fled the scene and managed to allude the police officers. However, when he stopped to catch his breath, he chose a spot within the view of a prison guard from Sing Sing Prison. The guard held him until police were able to make the arrest.

If there's a moral to this story, it may go like this: When fleeing the scene of a crime, mind where you choose to flee.

****

Here's a case where a man's quest for romance led him straight to the police.

Aron Morrison walked into a liquor store and attempted to secure a date with the clerk before absconding with a bottle of vodka. When the police arrived, the clerk gave the police a note from Aron, which included his name and phone number.

But rest easy, Aron. Your bumbling attempt to secure a date and a free drink doesn't come close to a Chicago bank robber's critical error.

Thomas Infante of Cary, Illinois robbed a bank in Chicago of $400 using a note written on the back of his own payslip. In his rush to leave the scene, Thomas forgot to retrieve the payslip. Agents from the FBI quickly tracked him down and solved the caper before supper.

****

Drug addicts are not always playing with a full deck.

In Silver Springs, Florida, three men broke into a home and left with three jars of what they thought was cocaine.

The drug addicts were elated with their big heist and attempted to celebrate with a good snort of their loot. They later discovered the contents of the jars were in fact the cremains of the theft victim's late husband and her two dogs.

****

Driving while intoxicated is never a good idea, but even under the influence of alcohol, a Fresno, California woman proved cooperative, and even helpful.

When asked if she was intoxicated, she apparently admitted she was, and then stated, "But my husband is right behind me, and he is drunker than I am."

****

Milton J. Hodges is apparently not a nudist. While attempting to rob an Orlando hardware store, Milton fled police and ran across the street where he jumped over a fence and into the Cypress Cove Nudist Resort and Spa.

Being one of the only people wandering around the resort with clothing, the police easily recognized him.

It looks like Milton forgot the wisdom of the adage, "When in Rome, do as the Romans."

****

You almost have to give Graham Price of South Wales a pass on this bank heist, as it appears he was only "borrowing" the money.

As an employee of the bank, Graham apparently had access to the safe. When police investigated the robbery, they found an IOU from Graham, admitting to the theft of 7 million pounds, with his signature at the bottom of the IOU.

****

Muggers must be far stupider than they look, as this street thug proved beyond any doubt.

A Good Samaritan observed an elderly man was being mugged. He raced to the victim's aid, and in the process roughed up the mugger. The mugger was so upset by the apparent assault, he called the police.

****

In York, Pennsylvania a bank robber met with several unexpected challenges.

When he approached the first teller window with his demands, the teller fainted in fear. He then moved to the next teller, who's cash drawer had not been stocked with cash. The third teller also claimed her cash drawer was empty.

Frustrated, the bank robber stomped out of the bank, stating he was going to write a letter of complaint. What a world, when even a bank robber can't get decent customer service.

****

Here's one more reason to avoid using email.

A German bank robber sent taunting emails to the police, ridiculing them for getting his description wrong, and suggesting he fled the scene on foot, when in fact, he used a getaway car.

Police arrested the bank robber that afternoon after connecting the email address to its owner.

****

Stories of thieves and armed robbers bragging about their heists on social media, or while sharing a drink with friends are commonplace. But in this case, a murderer revealed himself with a tattoo.

In Pico Rivera, California, a four year old murder case remained unsolved until a man was arrested for petty theft. During the booking photo, police noticed the thief wore an elaborate tattoo.

Upon closer examination, the police noticed the tattoo was a visual depiction of the murder scene.

Killers often keep souvenirs of their horrific acts, but in this case, the permanent nature of a tattoo marked the killer's undoing.

****

Counterfeiting U.S. currency is a serious crime, and even the best of the lot are challenged to match the right paper and ink and detailed engraving to reproduce passable bills.

In Memphis, Tennessee a restaurant customer tried to pass a counterfeit hundred dollar bill. He was undoubtedly proud of his creation, but made one fatal error…the hundred dollar bill featured the portrait of Abraham Lincoln.

In U.S. currency, Lincoln's portrait is on the five dollar bill. The hundred dollar bill features Benjamin Franklin.

****

Cattle rustling is not limited to the Wild West.

In a rural community in South Georgia, two men decided they would like to fill their freezer with a side of beef.

But rather than go to a butcher or meat market, they drove their four door sedan down a country road until they found a herd of cattle innocently minding their own business.

The cattle rustlers picked out the largest cow in the herd and shot her. They then did their best to butcher the cow and place the beef quarters in the trunk of the car.

To celebrate their theft and inhumane killing of the cow, they stopped at a convenience store to buy beer and cigarettes. While in the store, a police officer drove up next to their car. The police officer noticed the car was riding very low, and when he looked closer, noticed blood dripping from the bottom of the trunk.

After calling for backup, police officers discovered the remains of the butchered cow in the trunk.

Is cattle rustling still a hanging offense?

Exact numbers are hard to come by, but according to ranchers in Texas and Oklahoma, as many as 10,000 head of cattle go missing every year. Not all of those may be attributed to rustling, but law enforcement has noted a 40% increase in rustling since 2020.

Bumbling Lawmakers

The only things dumber than a bumbling burglar are the bizarre laws written by our elected dear leaders. J. Edgar Hoover once claimed he could find a reason to arrest any citizen, at any time. And considering some of the bizarre laws on the books at the city, state, and federal level, he may have been right.

According to Title 13, Chapter 33 of Arizona state law, it is illegal for a vendor to adjust the settings on crane arcade games, also known as claw machine games, to make it impossible to win a prize. Apparently, however, setting the tension on the crane fingers to the point where it is 'pert near impossible to win, is okay.

It is also illegal to misrepresent the value of the prizes a player may win.

Modern arcade crane games are electronic devices, which may be easily manipulated to ensure the vendor makes a profit. And that's okay, provided the player understands it's a game of chance, and approaches the game with an attitude of "having fun," as opposed to landing a bargain on a stuffed animal.

Claw machines are actually dwindling in popularity in America, but remain a quintessential favorite in Japan. The Sega Shinjuku Kabukicho in Shinjuku, Tokyo, holds the world record on claw machines, with 477 crane games in its arcade.

Japan is also home to the world's largest crane game. The glass enclosure is 12 feet tall and 10 feet wide and deep. The stuffed animal prizes are typically over 4 feet. It costs about $3.60 to play.

****

In Little Rock, Arkansas it is against the law to sound a car horn after 9 p.m. at any establishment that serves food and/or drink.

While the law sounds bizarre and arcane on the surface, it may actually be based on a sensible noise reduction initiative. Prior to the McDonald brothers changing the way customers ordered and received food at hamburger joints in the 1950s, customers would drive up, park, and honk their horn to get the attention of a car hop waitress…sometimes on roller skates.

Any person with the bad luck to live within a mile of a drive-thru restaurant would find themselves being serenaded by blaring horns long into the night.

****

If you live in Hong Kong, do NOT get caught cheating on your wife. Apparently, it is legal for a wife to kill her cheating husband…provided she uses her bare hands.

In Hong Kong, a wife needs only to demonstrate a "preponderance of probability" that her husband cheated on her.

Meanwhile, in Samoa it is illegal for a man to forget his wife's birthday.

****

Get this men. If you live in Switzerland it is illegal for you to urinate standing up after 10 p.m. Strange? Maybe not.

Given men's propensity for forgetting to put the seat of the toilet down after use, it's no surprise that women would object to midnight runs to the toilet ending with a cold soggy seat on the toilet rim.

****

When visiting Milan, Italy, don't forget to smile.

Apparently, an archaic law is still in effect there, that requires people to smile at all times, unless while visiting the hospital or attending a funeral.

****

According to West Virginia Code 17C-14-6, it is illegal to sing or whistle while operating a motorized vehicle.

****

In Singapore you can be fined for not flushing a public toilet, and even caned or imprisoned for chewing gum in public.

Singapore is famous for its strict cleanliness and hygiene laws and comes down hard for smoking, jaywalking, and littering, as well as drug use.

In Singapore, police can conduct random drug tests on citizens and tourists, with no cause or provocation required.

****

New York is not exempt from austere, and possibly outdated, laws.

- Keeping more than 4 dogs is prohibited.
- It is illegal to jump off a building.

- It's against the law to keep an elephant in your bathtub.

- It's illegal to a carry an ice cream cone in your pocket on Sundays.

- Taking selfies with lions and tigers is prohibited.

- Tying a giraffe to a light pole is illegal.

- It's illegal to frown at a police officer.

****

A proposed bill in Oklahoma will make it illegal to text any person, other than one's husband or wife, a sexually explicit message. In other words, no sexting allowed.

But how would such a law be enforced? And would it depend upon recipients of such messages turning the sender in to police?

****

In the state of Washington it is illegal for store owners to hypnotize passersby on the street.

Like most arcane and oddball laws, something must have happened to generate interest in creating a law to begin with.

For example, in the case of tying your giraffe to a light pole, at one time, a travelling circus may have tied one of its giraffes to a light pole. The giraffe may have resisted, causing damage to the pole, followed by the loud cry of a concerned citizen shouting, "there ought to be a law," leading J. Edgar Hoover to correctly surmise, "If I want you, I can get you."

Bumbling Insurance Claims

The following stories from actual insurance claims do not necessarily rise to insurance fraud, and while they may not show intent to commit a crime, the excuses offered to various insurance underwriters illustrate how easy it is to appear stupid, nonetheless:

- "I was just driving. I glanced over and took one look at my mother-in-law and drove off the cliff."
- "I backed out of my driveway and a bus hit me. The bus was running five minutes early."
- "I got into an accident because I had one eye on the truck in front of me, one eye on a pedestrian, and the other on the car behind me. It was not my fault."

- "The car in front of me hit a pedestrian. He got up, so I hit him again."
- "I collided with a parked truck coming the other way."
- "A pedestrian hit me and went under my car"
- "An invisible car came from nowhere and hit me, then vanished."
- "I was on my way home, minding my own business when I turned into the wrong driveway and hit a tree I don't have."
- "The guy driving the other car was all over the road. I had to swerve several several times before I manged to hit him."
- "I was sure the pedestrian would never make it to the other side of the road when I hit him."

Insurance companies in America receive over 3.5 million claims per year. The average homeowner's claim in 2022 was for $8,787, mostly from property damage and theft.

The bottom line is this: Whether you are a criminal contemplating the 100 different ways you could screw up a murder, or a lawmaker warping good intentions into sheer stupidity, be careful. The ghost of J. Edgar Hoover may be watching.

And if the day ever comes when temptation drives you to the edge of legality, don't be surprised if you find yourself immersed in the next "Trial of the Century."

Life in the Big House

Convicted felons are typically incarcerated in state and federal penitentiaries for varying lengths of time, depending upon their crimes, criminal history, and judicial discretion based on case precedent.

According to the World Prison Brief, the United States leads the world, with 25% of all incarcerated persons worldwide. Here are the number of persons imprisoned in the top five prison population nations around the world:

- United States 2,068,800
- China 1,690,00

- Brazil 811,707

- India 478,600

- Russia 471,490

Based on population, here are the rates of persons imprisoned per 100,000:

- United State 629

- Rwanda 580

- Turkmenistan 576

- El Salvador 564

- Cuba 510

Other than a couple African nations with sketchy judicial systems and statistics, Iceland maintains the lowest percent of imprisoned persons at 29 per 100,000 people.

Around the world, well over 90%, and 99% in many nations, of all prisoners are male. In the United States, 90% of all prisoners are male. Hong Kong has the highest percentage of female inmates versus male inmates. 81% of all prisoners in Hong Kong are male, leaving 19% of the prison population female. So, when visiting Hong Kong, take care not to mess with the women.

As a microcosm of the entire nation, California's prison population and offenses are interesting to true crime buffs. The following information is available online at the California Department of Corrections and Rehabilitation (CDCR). According to CDCR, the projected prison population for 2024 is 92,244. California has a population of 38.9 million. 2.3% of California's population is behind bars.

Breakdown of crimes committed by CDCR inmates. Note, some inmates are incarcerated with multiple offenses. Also, not all of the lower percentage crimes are detailed below.

- Murder 1.9%
- Robbery 9.6%
- Assault 24%
- Rape .6%
- Kidnapping .6%
- Burglary 12.2%
- Theft and Vehicle Theft 8.3%

- Drug Possession 14.9%
- DUI 2.7%
- Weapon Possession 8.4%

Interestingly, the highest category includes assault, which also includes the charge of assault with a deadly weapon. CDCR does not delineate assault with battery, but based on prisoners guilty of assault, and incarcerated for that crime, they most likely caused bodily harm to their victims.

A prison is a city unto itself, and aside from prison populations and the types of crimes committed by convicted felons, one may wonder about the best and worst prisons around the world, and even which prisons are the largest, ugliest, meanest, or most corrupt. So, here goes.

Sabaneta, Venezuela

Considered one of the most dangerous and disgusting prisons in the world, Sabaneta imprisons 3,700 inmates, in a space designed for 700.

But overcrowding is the least of its problems. With a guard to inmate ratio of 150:1, there is little chance to control the shenanigans of prison life within the walls of Sabaneta. Murder and abuse are common place, and riots can occur within a blink of an eye.

In 1994, a brutal riot left the building scorched black from fires, and resulted in the death of 108 inmates. More recently, a riot in 2013 left 16 inmates murdered.

Like any prison, Sabaneta has a pecking order. If a prisoner does not have the right status or connections, or the clout to assert authority within the prison, he will find himself forced to pay other inmates for a place to sleep and water to drink. And don't bother complaining. Most of the guards within the prison are actually inmates themselves, armed to the teeth.

Former Venezuelan president Hugo Chavez once stated, "Sabaneta is the gateway to the fifth circle of hell."

Rikers Island, New York

Rikers is technically a jail, not a prison. It is designed for temporary incarceration while inmates await trials and transfer to other prisons. Despite its mission, Rikers Island is frequently ranked among the top five worst prisons in the world.

Rikers Island is a 413 acre island in the Bronx area of New York City. As a side note, New York City is comprised of five Boroughs: The Bronx, Brooklyn, Manhattan, Queens, and Staten Island.

In an article dated 29 December 2023, *The New York Times* labeled Rikers Island the state's largest mental institution, an apparent reference to the state's tendency to house developmentally disabled and potentially criminally insane people there, with little to no legal representation, and a stark disregard for due process.

- Rikers Island is named after Abraham Rycken who first claimed the island in 1664.
- The island was originally only 100 acres, but was expanded to 413 acres using convict labor, with garbage and ash used as landfill.

- The garbage dump known as Rikers Island was turned into a jail in 1932.

- Rikers Island inmates are used to perform burials on neighboring Hart Island, where over 1 million people are buried.

- Rikers Island operates a prison farm on the island, under the auspices of a vocational training program.

- Rikers Island is often unidentified on New York City maps. Anti-incarceration activists accuse officials of attempting to hide the truth about mass incarceration from the public.

- During the Civil War, Rikers Island was used as a training base, as well as a prisoner of war camp.

- Since Rikers Island was built on a garbage dump, methane leaks from the decomposing garbage give the area a foul smell.

- Rikers Island inmates operate an 11,000 square foot bakery used to make bread for the prisoners. Their most popular creation is carrot cake.

- The ground beneath Rikers Island is constantly shifting and settling, creating havoc for building structure and plumbing integrity.

- To this day, many people refer to Rikers Island as the world's largest penal colony, reminiscent of the French penal colonies portrayed in the movie, *Papillon*.

Bang Kwang Prison, Bangkok, Thailand

Bang Kwang, also known by locals as the Bangkok Hilton, is notorious for prisoner abuse and ridiculously long sentences for petty crimes.

For example, in Thailand it is against the law to step on Thai currency because the currency includes an image of the King.

In Thailand it is illegal to drive a vehicle without a shirt, you cannot leave your house without underwear on, it is highly illegal to disrespect the Royal Family in any way, tourists are prohibited from displaying the flag of their homeland, littering is a major crime, owning over 120 playing cards is against the law, and you cannot speak into a microphone in any language other than Thai.

Considering how strict Thailand is with minor offenses like not wearing your underwear, or owning more than two decks of cards, is it any wonder their prison system would rank among the worst in the world?

- Bang Kwang prison was built in the 1930s, with a projected inmate capacity of 3,500.
- Currently, the prison has over 8,000 inmates, with most inmates serving 25 year sentences.
- 10% of its inmates are on death row.
- Bang Kwang death row inmates all have shackles permanently welded around their ankles.

Criminal Oddities

The U.S. Census Bureau recently claimed up to 40% of households in America fail to complete their census forms on time, and require personal follow up visits. But how does the Census Bureau know what they *don't* know?

Could crime statistics be the same? How many break-ins, muggings, assaults, bashed car windows, and graffiti tagged fences and walls go unreported? That said, the government loves to track crime statistics. The following is a random selection of criminal oddities, crime statistics, brief fun facts, and other true crime related data you may find interesting.

Death Row: According to the Death Penalty Information Center, females represent only 3.6% of total executions in America, with the first recorded execution of a woman occurring in 1632. Over the years, 576 total women have been executed in America. Officially, 16,047 men and women have been executed by the state in American history, as of 31 December 2022.

Executions in America: Since the Supreme Court allowed states to resume executions in 1976, Texas has led the nation in executions with 586, as of 31 December 2023. Texas averages 7-10 executions per year, so this number is bound to change.

Juvenile Hall Records: According to the Office of Juvenile Justice and Delinquency Prevention, over the course of a year, 500,000 youths will enter juvenile detention facilities in America, with approximately 36,000 being held in custody at any given time.

The Killer Giant: The Co-ed Killer, named Ed Kemper, stands 6'9" tall. When he was arrested on 24 April 1973, he was standing inside a phone booth. When police ordered him to raise his hands, the roof of the phone booth restricted his ability to raise his hands much higher than his head.

Failure Galore: According to the FBI, there are approximately 15,000 homicides each year in America, with a solved or resolved rate of 60%. Sadly, this rate is among the worst in the world.

Serial Killers…They're Everywhere: The FBI believes there are approximately 50 active serial killers in America at any time. An expert homicide investigator and serial killer tracker named Thomas Hargrove believes the number is much higher. According to Hargrove, there are at least 2,000 active serial killers in America today.

Ed Gein Macabre Creations: A real life character from the edge of insanity named Ed Gein was the inspiration for characters like Norman Bates in Psycho and Leatherface in The Texas Chain Saw Massacre. Gein created household items like lampshades and masks from human skin, and was fond of grave robbing. Gein was also known as the Butcher of Plainfield, Wisconsin.

The Black Dahlia Murder: The murder of Elizabeth Short, known as the Black Dahlia, on 15 January 1947 remains unsolved. Her body was found mutilated and bisected in a vacant lot in Los Angeles.

Short earned the Black Dahlia nickname from the press, who noted she routinely wore black clothes, and because a popular movie at the time was called, Blue Dahlia. Following the discovery of her body, police were able to identify her in 55 minutes using a relatively new FBI fingerprint database. Short had applied for a job on a military base and her prints were on file.

The Zodiac Killer's Cryptic Messages: The Zodiac Killer, active in the late 1960s and early 1970s in the San Francisco, California area, sent cryptic ciphers to newspapers, taunting law enforcement. Some of these codes remain unsolved, as well as the identity of the killer.

Ted Bundy's Charming Persona: Ted Bundy, a notorious serial killer, was known for his charm and good looks. He often lured his victims by feigning injuries and seeking their help. During his trial, the prosecution noticed the jury was falling for Bundy's charm routine. Near the conclusion of the trial the prosecutor intentionally goaded Bundy until Bundy's temperament got the best of him. His violent courtroom eruption revealed the true character of the man and led to his conviction.

The Tylenol Murders: In late 1982, someone tampered with Tylenol capsules on store shelves in the Chicago, Illinois area. The perpetrator laced Tylenol capsules with potassium cyanide, leading to seven deaths. The perpetrator was never caught, and it led to widespread changes in packaging and tamper-evident seals evident in virtually every packaged food product purchased to this day.

The Boston Strangler: Albert DeSalvo confessed to being the Boston Strangler, responsible for the deaths of 13 women in the early 1960s. However, doubts remain about the accuracy of his confession. It is believed The Boston Strangler gained access to women's apartments by disguising himself as a plumber or gas inspector. He was arrested on 27 October 1964, and was stabbed to death by an inmate for reportedly selling drugs to other inmates for less than the established prison black market price on 25 November 1973.

The Unabomber's Manifesto: Ted Kaczynski, the Unabomber, sent a manifesto to newspapers outlining his anti-technology beliefs. His brother recognized the writing style and helped the FBI secure Ted's capture. Kaczynski's brother donated the reward money to the families of Ted's victims. Ted died of apparent suicide in prison at the age of 81 on 10 June 2023.

The Lindbergh Kidnapping: The 1932 kidnapping and murder of Charles Lindbergh Jr., the son of aviator Charles Lindbergh, led to the famous trial and execution of Bruno Hauptmann. Hauptmann was electrocuted on 3 April 1936.

The Clutter Family Murders: The brutal murder of the Clutter family of four in Holcomb, Kansas, in 1959, was chronicled in Truman Capote's book, *In Cold Blood*. Capote's research assistant was Harper Lee, author of *To Kill a Mockingbird*.

The Great Train Robbery: In 1963, a gang of robbers in the UK stopped a Royal Mail train and stole 2.6 million pounds, or about 50 million pounds in today's money. Most of the gang was eventually captured.

The D.B. Cooper Mystery: In 1971, a man using the alias D.B. Cooper hijacked a plane, received a ransom, and parachuted out somewhere between Utah and Oregon, disappearing without a trace.

California Death Row: California reinstated capital punishment in 1978 following a Supreme Court ruling in 1976 that allowed states to conduct executions. Since then, 13 death row inmates in California have been executed, 82 have died from natural causes, and 27 have died by suicide.

The 1993 World Trade Center Bombing: Before the 9/11 attacks, the World Trade Center was targeted on 26 February 1993 when a truck bomb exploded in the parking garage, killing six people and injuring over 1,000.

The "Grim Sleeper" Serial Killer: Lonnie Franklin Jr., dubbed the "Grim Sleeper," was responsible for a series of murders in Los Angeles. He targeted young black women, reportedly killing 10 between the years 1984 to 2007, and was arrested on 7 July 2010. Franklin died of unknown causes in San Quentin State Prison on 28 March 2020. Franklin's preferred method of killing his victims was by gunshot. He photographed his deceased victims and kept the pictures in his garage as trophies. He earned the name Grim Sleeper due to his long breaks between murders.

The Oklahoma City Bombing: On 19 April 1995, Timothy McVeigh bombed the Alfred P. Murrah Federal Building in Oklahoma City, using a concoction of chemical fertilizers. The blast killed 168 people and injured 680. Timothy McVeigh was executed under federal jurisdiction on 11 June 2001, the first federal execution in 38 years. By Death Row time standards, McVeigh did not spend much time waiting for his appointment with the needle.

The Atlanta Child Murders: Wayne Williams was convicted of killing two adults, and suspected of killing up to 24 children in the Atlanta area between 1979 to 1981. He was arrested 21 June 1981 and found guilty of murder. He received a life sentence and is up for parole in November 2027. To date, the surviving family members of the 24 murdered children have no closure.

The "Son of Sam" Killer: David Berkowitz, also known as the Son of Sam, terrorized New York City in 1976-1977, claiming six lives and leaving behind chilling letters. Berkowitz notoriously blamed the murders on his neighbor's demon possessed dog who told him to kill.

The Hillside Stranglers: In a rare case of serial killers working as a team, and not as loners, Cousins Kenneth Bianchi and Angelo Buono Jr. were convicted of kidnapping, raping, and murdering several women in Los Angeles in the late 1970s.

The Anthrax Attacks: In 2001, letters containing anthrax spores were mailed to media outlets and government offices, killing five people and causing widespread fear. In one memorable case, NBC News Anchor, Tom Brokaw, received a tainted letter, and openly discussed the case on air. At one point, he held up a bottle of Ciprofloxacin, a medication used to fight possible anthrax exposure, and said, "Until we know otherwise, in Ciprofloxacin we trust." The anthrax attacks perpetrator's identity remains unknown.

The Big Con

The great carnival and circus promoter of the 19th Century, P.T. Barnum, once said, "The common man, no matter how sharp and tough, actually enjoys having the wool pulled over his eyes, and makes it easier for the puller."

Similarly, Mark Twain talked about how con men and pranksters moved about the Wild West "humbugging" the pioneers and settlers. For the most part, people accepted a humbug as entertainment, and accepted the loss of a little change for the purchase of a bottle of snake oil, or the brief distraction from the boredom of pioneer life on the prairie, as the price of entertainment.

But following the horror of two world wars, a depression, and the prevalence of gun running outlaws like Al Capone, John Dillinger, and Baby Face Nelson, the humor once found in a little con or scam was gone. And as the Big Con became more sinister, the stakes were raised, to the point where a single con could take everything you owned by simply answering your phone or replying to an email.

For example…

"Hello. This is Officer Matthew Arnold of the Bureau of Internal Revenue, Criminal Division. I am calling about back taxes you owe and have contacted your local Department of the Sheriff's Office concerning your case."

What a load of croc.

The call is designed to scare you into calling them back, where you will be led through a litany of lies, ending with you buying a variety of cash redeemable gift cards and mailing them to their "clearing" house address.

Notably, the IRS is called the Internal Revenue Service. Your IRS contact person is known as an Agent, not an Officer. And local law enforcement only gets involved when a legal court order may require their assistance in helping the IRS confiscate your property. Also, the IRS does not cold call taxpayers. If you owe the IRS money, they will send you a letter, advising you of a pending audit, with the opportunity to meet an agent in person to review your tax liability. And of course, the IRS deals in currency, not gift cards.

According to industry experts, cons just like this collect billions of dollars from intimidated and impressionable people every year. In fact, an organization called True Caller, believes up to 59 million Americans fall victim to scams just like the one described above each year, and the Associated Press estimates losses to individual consumers amounted to $5.5 billion in 2022. Make no mistake, cyber, telephone, banking, investment, and email scams are big business.

Adding to the confusion and potential for fraud, artificial intelligence now makes it possible for scammers to replicate the voice of a friend or family member. What would you do if you received a call from a person that sounds exactly like your son? He claims he is stranded, or in jail, and needs money sent by Western Union immediately. Most people would send the money.

Fast Facts

- 59% of scam victims are male.
- The majority of victims are aged 35-44, but elderly people are con artists' primary target.
- The FBI Internet Crime Complaint Center (IC3) received over 790,000 complaints in 2020. This number is only a fraction of the total of scam attempts, as most of us do not report spam telemarketer calls and spam email.
- The top three internet scam complaints included phishing, extortion, and non delivery of product scams.
- During 2020, the IC3 received 28,500 COVID 19 related complaints related to vaccine and treatment scams.

At the individual level, scams can be devastating to the victim and his or her family. But some of the biggest cons have impacted entire communities, and even nations, such as counterfeit war bonds, stock market "pump and dump" schemes, and various Ponzi schemes.

Here are a few more cons of interest from the annals of true crime trivia.

The Fake Nurse of the 1918 Flu Epidemic

Julia Lyons was not a nurse. However, that did not stop her from using the 1918 Flu Epidemic to her advantage. Disguised as a nurse, she offered home care services for people sickened by the flu. She apparently charged exorbitant rates for her services, and commonly charged her patients hundreds of dollars for prescriptions worth a fraction of the price.

While the amount of money Lyons made from her scheme does not approach the levels of contemporary phone, email, and pyramid schemes, the act of offering fraudulent medical care for people in crisis was repugnant.

The Eiffel Tower Salesman

Victor Lustig was a notorious counterfeiter and conman, who served time in Alcatraz. However, prior to landing in Alcatraz, Lustig developed a scheme to sell the Eiffel Tower.

In 1925, Lustig forged documents to make it look like he had the official power to sell the Eiffel Tower for scrap iron. Using his fraudulent identity, he set up meetings with scrap iron buyers and implied he would award the scrapping rights to anyone that paid him a bribe.

His primary target was a man named Andre Poisson. After taking Poisson's money (70,000 Francs), Lustig fled France, but returned to repeat the con when he discovered Poisson was too embarrassed to report the scam.

Lustig was arrested on 10 May 1935 in New York for counterfeiting. While he denied the claim, a key in his possession led police to a train station locker where Lustig had stashed $51,000 in counterfeit bills, as well as the plates used to produce the bills.

Lustig was sentenced to Alcatraz, and died in 1947 of pneumonia.

The First Con Man

In 1849 New York City, a man named William Thompson approached strangers on the street, and by gaining their confidence, managed to rob them of money and jewels.

Thompson's scheme was simple. He dressed and acted in a genteel manner and used his appearance and mannerisms to strike up conversations with upper class people he met while walking in various parks. Thompson would present himself as a friend or acquaintance and convince his mark to loan him a watch or piece of jewelry…which he never returned.

Local newspapers were soon referring to Thompson as "The Confidence Man," a title that came to be known as "con man." In 1857 Herman Melville wrote a novel entitled, *The Confidence Man* that many believe was inspired by Thompson's swindling.

Famous Last Words

There is a tradition whereby a condemned prisoner is allowed to make a final statement before being executed. Many of the condemned use this time to ask for forgiveness, to apologize, or say something of relevance to his or her victims' families.

But not always.

Here is a sampling of odd, spooky, irreverent, and bizarre famous last words.

Thomas J. Grasso: Grasso was executed on 20 March 1995 for strangling an elderly woman with her Christmas tree lights. He then robbed her for $8 and her television set, which he apparently sold for $125. Prior to dying, Grasso stated, "I did not get my Spaghetti-Os, I got spaghetti. I want the press to know this."

Sarah Good: Sarah was a victim of the Salem Witch Trials. She was accused of witchcraft because she did not attend church regularly, and was "surly." Sarah lost her inheritance due to the inheritance laws of the time that gave nothing to female survivors of an estate. Reduced to poverty, she was left to beg in the streets. She eventually married, but her husband was an indentured servant and also penniless. During her trial, Sarah's husband testified against her, claiming she was negligent in her wifely duties. She was hanged on 29 July 1692. In her last words she stated, "I am no more a witch than you are a wizard, and if you take away my life, God will give you blood to drink."

Vincent Gutierrez: Gutierrez was executed on 28 March 2007 for killing a man during a carjacking.

His last words included a nervous attempt at humor, "Where's my stunt double when you need one?"

Carl Panzram: Panzram was executed on 5 September 1930, after confessing in his autobiography of killing 21 people and raping over 1,000 men and boys. Police were unable to prove all of his confessed murders and rapes, but apparently enough to warrant the death penalty. In his last words, he cussed at the prison guards and said, "Yes, hurry it up! I could kill a dozen men while you're screwing around!"

Robert Charles Towery: Towery was executed on 8 March 2012 for strangling a man during a home invasion back in 1991. Towery apparently had a passion for Harley-Davidson motorcycles, and managed to send a message to his family by saying, "I love my family. Potato, potato, potato." For those of us who do not appreciate the sound of older motorcycles, the Harley is famous for what they call a potato-potato sound. His last words told his family he was okay. Sadly, his victim was not okay.

George Harris: Harris was executed on 13 September 2000 for killing a man in a dispute over the rightful ownership of two machine guns. Harris used his last opportunity to share his wisdom with the world to say, "Somebody needs to kill my trial attorney." It's not known if Harris was serious about the death threat, or just displaying a bizarre sense of humor. What is evident, however, is the classic example of many condemned prisoners where they blame the system, or even the victim, for their predicament.

Robert Charles Comer: Comer was apparently the epitome of a die hard Raiders fan. He was executed on 22 May 2007 for raping a camper and murdering another in 1987. In his last words he stated, "Go Raiders."

Robert Drew: Drew met his maker on 2 August 1994 after being convicted of stabbing a 17 year old to death. With yet another strike at the system that condemned him, Drew stated, "Remember, the death penalty is murder."

Bennie Demps: Demps was executed on 7 June 2000 for murdering three people in 1976. In his last words, Demps stated, "They butchered me back there. I was in a lot of pain. They cut me in the groin; they cut me in the leg. I was bleeding profusely. This is not an execution, it is murder." His last words refer to the difficulty prison officials had in finding a vein for the lethal injection needle insertion. According to official records, it took three attempts to set the needle. Anti death penalty activists claimed the three jabs were administered in retribution for his three victims, and constituted cruel and unusual punishment.

Gary Gilmore: Gilmore is a rare example of the convicted killer who admits his mistakes and asks the state to execute him. Gilmore was executed by firing squad in Utah on 17 January 1977 for the murder of two people. His last words, "Let's do it." A 1982 movie entitled *The Executioner's Song* with Tommy Lee Jones, was based on the Gilmore case.

Jimmy Glass: Glass was executed on 12 June 1987 for robbing and murdering a couple on Christmas Eve. His last words, "I'd rather be fishing." Too bad he didn't go fishing that Christmas Eve.

Grover Cleveland Redding: Redding was executed 24 June 1921 for apparently causing the deaths of two people during a riot. His last words, "I have something to say, but not at this time."

Karla Faye Tucker Brown: Karla was executed on 3 February 1998 after being convicted of killing two people with a pickaxe during a burglary. Her last words: "I am going to be face to face with Jesus now... I love you all very much. I will see you all when you get there... I will wait for you."

Saddam Hussein: After ruling Iraq and leading his nation to war with Iran, and then subsequently with the "world" after invading Kuwait, Hussein was hanged on 30 December 2006. His last words were from the Islamic faith. "There is no God but Allah and Muhammad is God's messenger."

George Engel: Engel considered himself an anarchist, or revolutionary, and was executed on 11 November 1887 after bombing the McCormick Plant in Chicago. In his last words he stated,

"Hurrah for anarchy! This is the happiest moment of my life."

James French: French died in the electric chair in Oklahoma on 10 August 1966. He was convicted of killing a motorist, and then later, he killed a fellow inmate. Using a play on his last name, French's last words were spoken to a journalist, "How about this for a headline for tomorrow's paper? French Fries."

Torrey Twane McNabb: McNabb was executed on 19 October 2017 after he shot and killed a Montgomery, Alabama police officer. In his last words he said goodbye to his family before turning his anger towards the state. "Mom, sis, look at my eyes. I got no tears. I am unafraid. To the state of Alabama, I hate you... I hate you. I hate you."

George Appel: Appel was executed on 9 August 1928 after shooting and killing a Brooklyn police officer while attempting to rob a restaurant. His last words were a play on words using his last name: "Well, gentlemen, you are about to see a baked Appel."

Barbara Graham: Barbara was executed on 3 June 1955 after murdering an elderly woman during a failed robbery attempt. Apparently, she felt she was innocent, as her last words questioned the veracity of her conviction. "Good people are always so sure they're right."

Robert Alton Harris: Harris was executed in the California gas chamber on 21 April 1992 for the murder of two teenage boys. In his last words, he stated, "You can be a king or a street sweeper, but everyone dances with the Grim Reaper."

Edward Ned Kelly: Ned Kelly was an infamous bushranger and escaped convict who lived in the wilds of Australia. He was accused of various murders and bank robberies, and was hanged on 11 November 1880. Not much for talking, Ned's last words were, "Such is life."

John Spenkelink: John was a petty thief who had previously served time before being convicted of killing another criminal in Florida. He was executed by electrocution on 25 May 1979. In a play on the adage, he who has the gold, makes the rules, John stated, "Capital punishment: Them without capital get the punishment."

Gary Burris: Burris was sentenced to death for the murder of a cab driver in Indianapolis. He died by lethal injection on 20 November 1997. Apparently, he was a *Star Trek* fan, as his last words were, "Beam me up."

Patrick Bryan Knight: Knight was executed by lethal injection on 26 June 2007 for the murder of two of his neighbors. While awaiting execution, Knight organized a contest to come up with the best joke to use in his last words. In the end, Knight used his own words and stated, "I said I was going to tell a joke. Death has set me free. That's the biggest joke. I deserve this. Go ahead, I'm finished."

Ted Bundy: Bundy was one of the most notorious serial killers in American history. During his killing spree, he took the lives of at least 36 women. He was executed by electrocution on 24 January 1989. His last words: "I'd like you to give my love to my family and friends."

Harry Harbord "The Breaker" Morant: Morant was an Australian military officer who was convicted of war crimes during the Second Anglo Boer War. He was executed by firing squad on 27 February 1902. His last words were directed to the firing squad: "Shoot straight, you bastards! Don't make a mess of it."

James W. Rodgers: Rodgers was executed by firing squad in Utah on 30 March 1960 for killing a man. Rodgers displayed a classic example of gallows humor when he chose these final words before facing the firing squad: "Bring me a bullet proof vest."

Jeffrey David Matthews: Matthews was found guilty of murdering a man (his uncle) and attempting to murder the victim's wife in a home invasion. Indicative of his viciousness, Matthews shot his male victim in the back of the head, execution style, and then cut the victim's wife's throat (it failed to kill her). After three stays of execution, the state of Oklahoma finally got the job done with a lethal injection on 11 January 2011. Matthews' last words were a humorous nod to the expected, yet non arrival, of another stay from the governor. "I think that governor's phone is broke. He hadn't called yet."

James Lewis Jackson: Jackson dealt with heavy drug addiction, and anger issues…both of which came to a head the night he murdered his wife and two stepdaughters by strangulation. Jackson was executed by lethal injection in the state of Texas on 7 February 2007. His last words were, "I'm ready to roll. Time to get this party started."

Johnny Frank Garrett: Garrett was arrested and convicted of the rape and murder of a nun in 1981 in the city of Amarillo. Critics of the charge pointed to Garrett's developmental disability and horrific childhood as reason to go easy on Garrett. Furthermore, a similar crime had been committed by a Cuban refugee, suggesting Garrett was innocent. Nevertheless, the state of Texas executed him on 11

February 1992. Garrett's last words were, "I'd like to thank my family for loving me and taking care of me. And the rest of the world can kiss my ass." Garrett also left a long letter behind, where he criticized and cursed all the officials involved in the investigation and trial, including the press and the jury. Interestingly, multiple people involved in the case, including the press, jurors, lawyers, witnesses, police, and even the medical examiner, died of suicide or cancer following Garrett's execution. Garrett's letter has come to be known as "The Curse Letter."

Francis 'Two Gun' Crowley: Crowley was arrested in New York City following a two hour shootout with police. The shootout marked the culmination of a three month crime spree. He was executed in the state of New York by electrocution on 21 January 1932. The 1930s era was marked by a slew of bank robbers, gang warfare, and bootlegging. Some of the more notorious criminals of the time included Bonnie and Clyde, Baby Face Nelson, Pretty Boy Floyd, John Dillinger, and Al Capone, among a bunch of others. Crowley's last words were, "You sons of bitches. Give my love to Mother."

Barney Olwell: In 1865 Orwell shot and killed a farmer who owed him $40. He was executed in San Francisco by hanging on 22 January 1866. Standing on the gallows, Olwell stated, "I don't know as I've got anything to say; I am going to be hanged, and don't want to make a stump speech."

Money Money Money

Money is money, and no matter what you call it, it remains, money.

From the first day money was invented as a tool for bartering, people have given it nicknames. One of the oldest nicknames for money in America, and still used today, is the word, Buck. It's origins date back to colonial America and may have been derived from the way deer skins, or buckskins, were often used in bartering.

Today, money may be known by a hundred different slang terms, including those listed below.

Bacon

Bringing home the bacon is a tireless expression denoting the bread winner's role in providing for his or her family. Like the words bread and dough, bacon suggests the close correlation between money and sustenance.

Bank

A bank is not just a place to store money. In the context of slang, having "bank" suggests having a large sum of money on hand. A person making a lot of money may be said to be , "making bank."

Bankroll

The word bankroll may be either a noun or a verb. In the case of bankrolling a friend or business partner, it serves as a verb, while the word bankroll by itself suggests a person has a large sum of money.

Benjamins, Benjis, and Dead Presidents

Calling money Benjamins, Benjis, and Dead Presidents is urban slang for currency. And while Alexander Hamilton on the ten dollar bill, and Benjamin Franklin on the hundred dollar bill, may not have been presidents, they do represent the Founding Fathers, and meet the criteria for urban slang.

Big One, Grand, Large

A Big One, Grand, or Large refers to a thousand dollars. So, ten Big Ones, ten Grand, or ten Large means ten thousand dollars.

Bread and Dough

Money is of course commonly accepted medium of exchange where printed notes are traded for the things we need and want. At the most basic level, we want food. And since bread is pretty much the most basic of foods, it makes since that bread can stand as a synonym for money.

Along those same lines, the word bread can be reduced to the dough used to make bread. The use of the word "dough" for money can be traced back to 1851.

Buck

Referring to paper currency as a buck or bucks, as in, "loan me five bucks," is the most common nickname for money in America. The term derives from the use of buckskins as a bartering tool.

C Note

The Roman numeral for 100 is C. A C Note is a hundred dollar bill.

Cake

A more valuable form of bread, or dough. As in, icing on the cake, used to denote a bonus or something extra.

Capital

Capital refers to the money used to make an investment, or the value of a company. In slang use, having the capital to organize and conduct a telemarketing scam may refer to the money needed to rent space, set up phone lines, buy computers, etc. In this context, capital may actually be the same as a grubstake.

Not necessarily a slang term when employed in a business context, but can also be used as slang to refer to any kind of money, not just capital.

Does that make cents? (See what I did there?)

Cha-Ching, Ka-Ching

The sound of a cash register ringing up a sale. It is often used to denote raking in the bucks, or completing a successful business venture or heist.

Cheese, Cheddar

Another word for money tied to food. In this case, cheese refers to a common USDA commodity given to welfare recipients. Guv-ment cheese. Guv-ment money. By the way, guv-ment cheese makes great grilled cheese sandwiches.

Chips

Traditionally, a chip is a plastic coin used in poker, denoting a predetermined money value. In slang use, a chip can also mean money. The expression, "when the chips are down," suggests money has been gambled or put at risk.

Chump Change

Urban slang for a small amount of money. A chump is a derogatory label applied to a person who is perceived to be of little value or significance.

Coin

Typically refers to a small amount of money. As in, "I don't have the coin to go out tonight." Or, "Can I borrow some coin?"

Dime

In the US, a dime is the coin worth ten cents. In slang terms, a criminal could say, "My old lady dropped a dime on me. Now I'm stuck here doing a nickel." Which means his ex dropped a coin into a payphone and ratted him out, resulting in his imprisonment for five years. Another use of the word dime can be used to deny financial responsibility for something, saying something like, "not on my dime."

Dinero

Dinero is a Spanish word for money. This was a popular term for money in the Wild West, suggesting the common use of Tex-Mex in the spoken language of the American Southwest. Mucho dinero is a way of saying, lots of money.

Dosh

A British slang term for money.

Fiver

Five bucks, as in, "I make a fiver for every case of beer I can steal." The word fiver is also used by a website called Fiverr that offers digital services for five dollars.

Folding Money

As opposed to coins, folding money refers to paper currency. The stuff you can fold and jam into a billfold or pocket.

Greenbacks

American currency is green. However, this term dates back to the Civil War when currency was printed black on the front and green on the back.

Grubstake

A term used by gold prospectors and entrepreneurs to denote the start up cash needed to start a venture. While the word, grub, suggests food, it can also mean the supplies and equipment needed to open a business or venture into the desert in search of gold.

Jackson

Andrew Jackson graces the front of the $20 bill. If a person said she has three Jacksons, she has $60.

Lettuce, Cabbage, Celery

Perhaps derived from the fact that lettuce, cabbage, and celery are green, matching the color of U.S. currency. It may also refer to money as a source of food…in this case a vegan's grocery haul.

Loot

Can either refer to the process of looting a store, or finding a pile of loot. In the context of money, loot is treasure or cash…often used when the proceeds are obtained through ill gotten means.

Lucre

Related to the word, lucrative. Lucre suggests an abundance of money, typically obtained through robbery, or as Webster's Dictionary claims, "shameful gain."

Moola, Moolah

Webster's Dictionary claims the use of the word moolah to denote money was first used in 1936. Its origins are unknown.

Nickel

Nickel is the base metal for the 5 cent coin. Used as slang for money it can mean $5 or $500 worth of something…especially in drug trades. In prison terms, a nickel can mean a five year sentence. Also, the term "double nickels" was often used to describe the 55 MPH speed limit.

Pesos

Pesos are the official currency of Mexico. It is sometimes used to refer to dollars as well, such as, "that's a lot of pesos."

Quid

The word quid refers to English Pounds. It's use dates back to the 1600s, although its origin is unclear. A quid is considered equal to one pound, or one hundred pence.

Riches, Loaded

An easy way to brag about the amount of money you have. Rather than saying, "I have 40 grand in the bank," you could just say "I'm rich." Or, "I have riches," and leave the exact amount up to the listener's imagination. Either way, riches suggests money…and lots of it. A variation on this theme is to suggest that a person is "loaded." That is, he or she is loaded with cash.

Salad

Another slang word derived from calling money lettuce, cabbage, celery, etc.

Sawbuck

A sawbuck is a ten dollar bill. The word was derived from the word buck, and the appearance of a sawhorse, whose legs resemble an X, from the Roman numeral meaning ten.

Scratch

Use of the scratch to denote money became popular in the early 20th century. Its origins are unknown, by may relate to the expression, "starting from scratch," which means with nothing. Another way of saying you are starting from scratch is to claim "we're opening this business on a shoestring," which suggests you are starting with very little money.

Shekels

Shekels is a Hebrew word, meaning weight. It is the Israel currency, and is common in biblical references.

Simoleon

Slang word for money popular among 1930s era gangsters. It was also used as the currency in the Popeye movie staring Robin Williams and Shelley Duvall. It is also a popular word for money in some board games.

Smackers

A term for dollars popular with elderly people in the urban East Coast area. Smackers suggest a stack of cash tall enough to smack somebody in the face with.

Stash

Refers to money you have stashed, or hidden. Also applies to drugs, as in a dope smoker's stash of marijuana.

Ten Spot

A ten-dollar bill.

Wad

A stack of cash rolled into a wad, like a roll of toilet paper. If a thief noticed a man holding a roll of money in his hand, he may think, "check out that wad of dough."

Wampum

Contemporary use of the word wampum generally refers to a stash of marijuana. However, its original use dates back to a collection of shells, trinkets, and other trade goods a Native American may possess.

Pub Trivia Crime Wave

The following is a rundown on popular, or common, crime related pub trivia questions (with answers) you may encounter.

Question: What famous vocalist was arrested in Miami in 1969 for allegedly exposing himself on stage?

Answer: Jim Morrison

Question: Jim Morrison was the leader singer for a 60s rock band called *The Doors*. When did Morrison die, and where is he buried?

Answer: Morrison died of heart failure, attributed to an apparent heroin overdose on 3 July 1971 while in Paris, France. He is buried at Père Lachaise Cemetery in Paris, near the grave sites of other famous celebrities, writers, and artists, including Oscar Wilde and Edith Piaf.

Question: Who was arrested in public toilets on Hampstead Heath in September 2008 for possession of illegal drugs?

Answer: George Michael

Question: In 2008, Ingrid Betancourt was released after being held captive by FARC guerrillas for 6 years. Where do FARC operate, and what do the letters in their name mean?

Question: What vehicle did Clyde Barrow from the Bonnie & Clyde gang prefer over all other?

Answer: A Ford V-8. The car Bonnie and Clyde died in was a 1934 Ford Fordor Deluxe sedan.

Answer: Colombia. The Revolutionary Armed Forces of Colombia. In Spanish, Fuerzas Armadas Revolucionarias de Colombia.

Question: President Abraham Lincoln was assassinated in 1865 by John Wilkes Booth. What was the name of the theater in Washington D.C. where Lincoln was shot?

Answer: Ford's Theater. The theater is owned and controlled by the National Park Service. Guided tours of the theater are available to this day.

Question: Ruth Ellis was the last female to be executed by hanging in Britain. What year did the hanging take place?

Answer: 1955

Question: What is the real name of the Paris, France serial killer known as Dr. Satan?

Answer: Dr. Marcel Petiot.

Question: The infamous serial killer Jack the Ripper was not always known by the name we know today. How was the killer known at the time of his crimes?

Answer: The White Chapel Murderer.

Question: In recent years, which criminal activity has been prevalent in the Red Sea and around the Horn of Africa?

Answer: Piracy.

Question: The Watergate scandal of the 1970s spelled the end to Richard Nixon's presidency. What date did he resign from office, and who replaced him?

Answer: Richard Nixon resigned his presidency on 8 August 1974. Gerald Ford replaced him as president, immediately.

Question: Charles Manson led a commune of hippies on a killing rampage in Southern California in the 1960s. After years of imprisonment, Manson died at Mercy Hospital in Bakersfield, California (still a prisoner). How old was Manson at his death?

Answer: Manson died of natural causes at 83.

Question: Hollywood and scandal are two words we often find together, sadly. In 1943 an iconic Hollywood star faced 3 charges of rape. He was eventually acquitted. What was the actor's name?

Answer: Errol Flynn.

Question: Johnny Depp portrayed a real life criminal in the 2009 movie called, Public Enemies. What infamous criminal did Depp portray?

Answer: John Dillinger. Dillinger was the focal point of J.Edgar Hoover's campaign to eliminate the 1930s era gangsters and bank robbers prevalent at the time. Hoover, assigned FBI agent Melvin Purvis to hunt down and kill Dillinger. Purvis completed his mission on the night of 22 July 1934, in Chicago.

Purvis also spearheaded investigations leading to the death of bank robbers Baby Face Nelson and Pretty Boy Floyd.

Question: Who did Leon Czolgosz assassinate in Buffalo, New York in 1901?

Answer: President McKinley.

Question: Mark Chapman killed John Lennon on 8 December 1980. What was the name of the famous apartment building in New York City where Lennon lived at the time of his death?

Answer: The Dakota.

Question: John Hinckley attempted to assassinate President Ronald Reagan on 30 March 1981. What is the name of the female movie star Hinckley claimed he did it for?

Answer: Jodie Foster.

Question: How old was Lee Harvey Oswald on the date of the John F. Kennedy assassination?

Answer: 24.

Question: Catherine Murphy is famous for being the last last woman to be burned at the stake in Britain on 18 September 1788. No, she was not a witch. What was her crime?

Answer: Counterfeit coin forging.

Question: Interpol is a European based international crime investigation agency, comparable to America's FBI, and cooperates with police forces in over 180 countries. It was founded on 7 September 1923. Where is the present HQ of Interpol?

Answer: Lyon, France.

Question: Which serial killer claimed he was commanded to kill by a demon that possessed his neighbor's dog?

Answer: David Berkowitz. Also known as, Son of Sam.

Question: Gangsters, bank robbers, and bootleggers were rampant in America during the 1930s. Where did the infamous gangster, Al Capone, establish his criminal organization?

Answer: Chicago.

Question: What crime was Al Capone eventually charged and convicted on?

Answer: Income tax evasion.

Question: Lord Haw Haw (William Joyce) was a despised Nazi propagandist during the Second World War. Throughout the war he broadcast radio messages from Berlin, designed to demoralize British and American soldiers. On what charges was Lord Haw Haw tried at the end of the war?

Answer: Treason. He was executed on 3 January 1946.

Question: When O.J.Simpson was convicted of armed robbery in 2008, it was 13 years to the day that he'd been acquitted for what?

Answer: Murder of Nicole Brown Simpson (Simpson's ex-wife) and Ronald Goldman on 12 June 1994.

Question: How many women are currently on Death Row in the American prison system?

Answer: 50.

Question: What two key character traits do psychopaths lack?

Answer: Empathy and remorse.

Question: We've all heard of criminals or killers being described as sociopaths or psychopaths. But, what's the difference?

Answer: Basically, a psychopath is a person who lacks remorse for the crimes he or she commits, and may take pleasure in manipulating others, or causing them pain (both physical and emotional). On the other hand, a sociopath is anti-social and may enjoy being rebellious or unconventional.

Question: Which American serial killer dressed up as a clown?

Answer: John Wayne Gacy.

Question: The St. Valentine's Day Massacre is associated with which 1930s era gangster?

Answer: Al Capone. The massacre on 14 February 1929 left seven members of the Irish North Siders gang, led by George Bugs Moran, dead. While never conclusively proven, members of the Italian Chicago Outfit gang, led by Al Capone, lined the men up against a wall and gunned them down. Rumors at the time suggested Chicago police were involved in the shooting, and helped kill the gang members out of revenge for their alleged involvement in the death of a police officer's son.

Question: Prior to be being called the Federal Bureau of Investigation, what name(s) did the FBI use?

Answer: Prior to 1935, the FBI was known as the Division of Investigation, and the Bureau of Investigation.

Question: Name the Army veteran who rigged an explosive device and blew up the Murrah Federal Building in Oklahoma City on 19 April 1995, killing 168 people.

Answer: Timothy McVeigh.

Question: On 22 December 1984 a so-called "vigilante" shot and seriously wounded four men on a New York subway who he claimed were attacking him. What is the shooter's name?

Answer: Bernard Goetz. Goetz faced multiple charges, including attempted murder, but was only convicted of carrying an unlicensed firearm. He served 8 months in prion for this crime. His trial was highly controversial, and set in motion a string of debates about the right to self-defense, and continues to impact conceal carry laws to this day.

Question: On 25 March 1911, a fire broke out in a New York City factory, resulting in the deaths of 146 people. Fire investigators found the factory owners had locked emergency exists to prevent the employees from taking unauthorized breaks. The owners were charged with manslaughter. What is the name of the factory where this fire occurred?

Answer: Triangle Shirtwaist Factory. Owners Max Blanck and Isaac Harris were charged with manslaughter, but were acquitted. In a subsequent wrongful death civil suit, the victim's families were awarded $400 per casualty. The last known survivor of the fire, Rose Freedman, died at the age of 107 in 2001. She survived the fire by following the factory owners to the roof of the building.

Crime As We Know It

Have you ever wondered about the difference between homicide, murder, and manslaughter? Or asked yourself why theft, robbery, and burglary are different?

If so, this in-depth discussion of crimes and criminal charges may help clarify things for you. Charges appear in alphabetical order.

Aggravated Assault

An assault may be as simple as touching another person, but to become an aggravated assault, the assault must cause bodily injury to another person, or include the use of a deadly weapon. Aggravated assault charges can be first degree, second degree, or third degree, depending upon the attacker's intent, weapon used, amount of injury the victim sustains, and even the state of mind of the attacker.

Enhancements for aggravated assault are often added when the victim is elderly, disabled, or pregnant. Hate crime enhancements may also be added if the attack was motivated by the victim's race, gender, or sexual orientation.

In 2022, the rate of aggravated assault in America was 268 cases per 100,000 of the population. Therefore, if you lived in a city with a population of 100,000, 268 citizens of your community may expect to be victims of an aggravated assault per year. In some of these cases, aggravated assault charges may be combined with other charges, such as disorderly conduct and domestic violence.

Aiding and Abetting, or Accessory

To charge a person with aiding and abetting, the court must prove that a crime was committed, the accused aided or counseled the person doing the crime, and the accused acted in a way that facilitated the crime.

An accessory to a crime is a person who knows a person committed a crime and took action to protect that person from arrest, trial, or punishment.

There's no proof of this, but many believe Bonnie Parker's role in the bank robberies and murders attached to the Bonnie and Clyde gang were as an accessory. That is, many witnesses claim she stayed in the car during bank robberies and acted as a lookout. In that case, she aided Clyde Barrow in his nefarious actions, and was an accessory to the crimes he committed.

Clyde would be charged as the principal offender, while Bonnie would be charged with aiding and abetting, as well as accessory.

In many states, being on scene and supporting the trigger puller in a murder makes the accessory to the murder just as guilty as the trigger puller. In other words, she was guilty by association.

Arson

Arson is the willful or deliberate burning of property, including buildings, cars, and fields or forests. Arson is considered a serious felony due to the dangers of setting fires, as well as the potential to commit insurance fraud or destroy physical evidence that may be used to prosecute other crimes.

Arson is further defined by a variety of different classes:

- First Degree: Setting fire to an occupied building that may threaten safety of its occupants.
- Second Degree: Setting fire to an unoccupied building or car.
- Third Degree: Setting fire to an open space or forest.
- Fourth Degree: Reckless starting of a fire that spreads and causes damage to property.
- Aggravated: The intentional setting of a fire that results in injury or death. Typically used as an enhancement to a charge of first or second degree arson.

In 2022, over 6,508 motor vehicles were intentionally set on fire. Arson cases that year totaled 36,274, with 13,147 being structure fires.

Assault/Battery

Assault and battery are often confused as the same offense. However, they are quite different.

An assault occurs when a person threatens another person to the extent that the victim believes he or she is imminent danger. Battery requires actual physical contact.

Assault elevates to aggravated assault when the threat of violence is carried out, resulting in injury to the victim.

An assault and battery charge may result from a person threatening to harm another person, and then intentionally doing something that causes bodily injury. Accidentally bumping into a person is not assault or battery, as the accused person did not intentionally bump into the victim. However, if the person is reckless or negligent, and his reckless behavior causes injury to another, he may be charged with battery.

Attempt

You may be charged with criminal attempt if you plan and take action to commit a crime, but fail to complete the crime. For example, if a man goes into a bank with the intent to rob the bank, but fails because the bank guard blocks his robbery attempt, he is not guilty of robbing a bank; however, he may be guilty of attempting to rob the bank.

Similarly, if a person intends to kill another person, but fails to complete the job (fortunately), he is not guilty of murder, but may be guilty of attempted murder.

Bribery

Bribery is the offer or acceptance of any exchange of something of value for influence over a government official.

In contrast to extortion, a bribe is an offer to reward action by a government official. Extortion is the threat of violence or punitive action if the government official does not comply with a desired decision or outcome.

For example, if a person threatens to burn a judge's house down with him in it if he does not rule in favor of the person extorting the judge, that person has committed extortion. If the same person offered to pay the judge for a favorable ruling, then that is bribery.

Burglary

Burglary is the unlawful entry into a home or place of business with the intent to commit theft. The burglary does not have to require breaking and entering, and may just involve walking through an open door.

Burglary is distinct from robbery in that burglary does not involve the threat of violence against a person. For example, entering a retail store after hours and emptying the beer cooler of its contents is burglary. If the criminal confronts the storekeeper and threatens to do bodily harm to the storekeeper unless the storekeeper gives him the beer, than that is robbery.

Burglary charges may range from a misdemeanor to a felony, depending upon the value of items stolen. A misdemeanor charge can land a thief in the county jail for up to one year. A felony charge can land the thief in state prison for up to three years.

Home invasion is one of the most common forms of burglary, and occurs over 1 million times per year in America.

Child Abandonment

Child abandonment occurs when a parent, guardian, or person given custodial care of a child fails to provide the child with a safe, supervised environment.

Examples of child abandonment include:

- Leaving an infant unattended or dropping the child off at a doorstep or other public or private place without first securing adult supervision for the child.
- Leaving a child home alone or in a car alone in a manner that poses risk to the child's health and safety.
- Leaving a child with another person without paying for, or arranging for his or her care.

- Refusing to provide for a child's basic needs, such as food, shelter, and medical care.

Most states have Safe Haven laws that allow a parent to legally drop their child off at designated places, such as fire stations, hospitals, schools, and churches. However, if the parent drops the child off in front of a school or other public place when no immediate care is available, the parent may still be guilty of child abandonment.

Most states also have Mandated Reporter laws that require teachers, doctors, counselors, day care providers, and social workers, among others, to immediately report any observed act or evidence of child abandonment, neglect, or abuse to the police.

Child Abuse

We all know child abuse when we see it, but this is its legal definition.

Any act, or the omission of an act, that creates a substantial risk to a child's health and safety. In other words, a person may be guilty of child abuse if his or her actions impose physical, mental, or emotional harm to a child. He or she may also be guilty of child abuse if their inaction causes a child to be exposed to physical, mental, or emotional harm.

For example, if a mother allows her boyfriend to physically harm her child, they are both guilty of child abuse. Of course, even the briefest visit to the family court system will show that every case of child abuse is complicated and specific to each situation. Judges in this area cannot simply point to case precedent and make rulings, as in adult criminal cases.

There are four basic stipulations to a charge of child abuse:

- The victim is a minor (usually under 18).
- The abuser must have acted purposefully, recklessly, or with understanding his or her action, or inaction, would cause harm.
- There must be a specific act or act of omission.
- The act, or omission, must cause harm, or pose substantial risk of harm, including physical, mental, or emotional.

Family court cases are intentionally kept secretive, so it's difficult to determine hard statistics regarding child abuse. What we do know, is that over 12,850 inmates in federal prisons are there stemming from child sex offenses. The federal government spends over $508 million per year to hold child predators in prison. Of course, not all child abuse rises to the level of sexual abuse, thankfully.

Somewhat unrelated, but still indicative of family court issues, according to the U.S. Census Bureau, 80% of child custody cases result in the mother winning custodial rights, with child support payments equaling approximately $390 per month, per child. The total amount of child support owed is highly variable, and depends upon a family's income and needs.

Child Neglect

Child neglect may be a passive form of child abuse, but it is also deadly. Nearly 2,000 children die each year in America due to neglect, and this does not include the emotional and mental strain this places on a child, and his or her ongoing psychological health as an adult.

Child neglect represents 76% of all child maltreatment cases. In contrast, physical abuse accounts for 16%, and sexual abuse accounts for 10%.

Child neglect is known as passive abuse, that is, a parent or person responsible for custodial care, fails to take action to secure a child's access to food, shelter, healthcare, and education. Impossible to measure or document, the subject of giving a child the love and support he or she deserves is also a significant part of child neglect.

Child Pornography

Child pornography is a highly distasteful and morally repugnant subject that is, nevertheless, pervasive around the world.

Legally, child pornography is called Child Sexual Abuse Material (CSAM). Child pornography charges include the production, distribution, or possession of pornographic material depicting a person under the age of 18.

People found guilty of child pornography charges face stiff penalties. On average, a person found guilty of producing child pornography can face 15 to 30 years in prison, with mandatory federal penalties for multiple offenses set at 35 years to life in prison. Those found guilty of possessing child pornography also face prison time.

There are 1,435 child pornography prisoners in the federal system, and 99% of all persons found guilty of creating, distributing, or possessing Child Sexual Abuse Materials serve time in prison.

Computer Crime

Hackers…they're everywhere.

Computer crime is like any other crime of theft or fraud, with the one exception being the criminal uses a computer to lighten your wallet. Examples of computer crime include:

- Gathering, collecting, and distributing national security information.
- Using a computer to dox or collect personal and proprietary information (company secrets).
- Gaining illegal access to a government or company owned computer or database.

- Accessing a computer to defraud another, or obtain valuable information.

- Intentionally planting a virus in a computer to destroy information or hold the computer and/or database ransom.

- Recklessly damaging a computer or database while intentionally and fraudulently gaining access to it.

- Obtaining and/or distributing passwords.

- Extortion using a computer, such as in ransomware.

One of the more common computer crimes individuals encounter are so-called phishing cons, where a criminal attempts to collect personal and financial information through emails. A classic example of this is the Nigerian Prince scam. In this case, a criminal sends thousands of spam emails with a tearjerker story about a lost inheritance or a chance to claim a financial windfall. The victim is offered a chance to "buy-in" to the lost money scam and is often sent worthless gift cards or fake securities in exchange for his or her investment, or banking information.

The best thing to do is not to even bother opening unsolicited emails.

American consumers lose over $4 billion per year to phishing and other retail level computer crimes. The amount lost by government agencies and corporations due to ransomware is incalculable.

Conspiracy

Conspiracy is a crime, even if the planned crime is not carried out. For example, when two or more people join forces to plan a robbery, they are all guilty of conspiracy to commit a crime.

Conspiracy charges are often used as enhancements to charges for other crimes. For example, if a drug dealer is arrested for distribution, he, and his associates may also face charges of conspiracy if it can be proven he coordinated with others to obtain and distribute illegal drugs.

Counterfeiting

Counterfeiting is often thought of as the illegal reproduction of fake currency. However, an even more prevalent crime of counterfeiting is the production of fake products under the name of a recognized and trademarked brand.

For example, a jersey counterfeiter may print and sell football jerseys using the trademark name of the NFL. By placing the NFL's official logo on the tag, and displaying a team's name and logo on the jersey without a license from both the NFL and the team, he or she is guilty of counterfeiting.

High end products like Rolex watches, Coach handbags, and Ralph Lauren polo shirts are common victims of counterfeit operations.

When purchasing products online or from a street vendor, be on the look out for tell tale signs of fraud like misspelled words in the title or description, poor packaging, and of course, the price.

If the deal looks too good to be true, it is probably fake.

Credit/Debit Card Fraud

Criminal credit and debit card fraud refers to the illegal and intentional act of obtaining, using, or attempting to use another person's credit or debit card information without their consent.

Credit and/or debit card fraud may include: identity theft, creation of fake cards, unauthorized transactions, trafficking in stolen goods, and various computer hacking crimes.

According to the Federal Trade Commission (FTC):

- Credit card fraud is the most common type of reported identity theft, with most complaints spurring from new credit card account requests.
- The FTC reports 46% of all reports to the FTC in 2022 were fraud related, totaling over 1.1 million reports.
- The FTC estimates American consumers lost $8.8 billion to fraud in 2022.
- The FTC received 441,000 credit card fraud reports in 2022, with the most reports coming from victims aged 30-39 years old.

One interesting way credit and debit card thieves are collecting information is the use of fake card scanners at gas pumps and store checkouts. Convenience stores are the most common places these fake scanners are installed. They are typically just a fake keypad and card reader that lies on top of the real store scanner. When a person slides his card and types his PIN on the keypad, the fake scanner records this information. The thieves can later retrieve the fake scanner and use the data collected to make fake cards.

Criminal Contempt of Court

Contempt of Court refers to a deliberate and willful act of disobedience, disrespect, or obstruction of the authority, dignity, or orders of a court, and occurs when a person engages in behavior that undermines or obstructs the administration of justice, while also showing disregard for the court's authority.

Criminal Contempt of Court is categorized as a criminal offense because it involves intentional actions that hinder the proper functioning of the judicial system. For example, if a lawyer speaks out of turn, or in a manner the judge deems inappropriate, he may be held in contempt of court. The judge in this case typically issues a bench ruling at the time of the event, and invokes a penalty of a fine, or in some cases, jail time, on the offender.

Cyber Bullying

Flaming or trolling another person online, such as in the comment section to a video or article, is common, and while hurtful, may not rise to the level of cyber bullying.

However, the repeated and intentional act of demeaning or insulting a person online, especially in the social media world, can be considered cyber bullying. Technically, cyber bullying is a form of harassment or intimidation that takes place online, involving the deliberate and repeated targeting of an individual with harmful, threatening, or demeaning content.

Cyber bullying may involve various tactics, such as spreading false information, posting offensive content, or using comments or images to socially isolate the victim. Of rising concern is the use of artificial intelligence and photo editing to create images that demean or falsely impugn victims.

According the Center for Disease Control, teenagers are especially vulnerable to cyber bullying, with 14.9% of minors claiming to have experienced cyber bullying. Over 13% of those who experience cyber bullying consider suicide, with many following through with suicide, or suicide attempts.

Disorderly Conduct

Disruptive, unruly, or offensive behavior in a public place that disturbs the peace-and order may be characterized as disorderly conduct. Typically, people charged with this crime have been engaged in a physical confrontation, playing loud music, or making offensive gestures or remarks towards other people.

Punishment is usually deemed a misdemeanor and results in a fine. More serious offenses, with enhancements like battery or vandalism can result in probation and jail time.

Disturbing the Peace

Similar to disorderly conduct, disturbing the peace implies a person has created a nuisance with noise, such as music and racing car engines in a residential area. Persons disturbing the peace are often given a verbal warning to tune things down a bit, but repeated offenses can result in a citation.

Domestic Violence

Domestic violence situations are among the most dangerous and volatile calls a police officer responds to. Technically, domestic violence involves acts within a household, family, or between partners, that cause fear, harm, or distress, and may lead to physical or mental injury, impairment, or endangerment.

According to national statistics:

- 10 million men and women experience domestic violence each year in America.
- 25% of all women and 11% of all men experience intimate partner violence ranging from physical violence, sexual violence, and stalking.
- 1 in 10 women have been raped by an intimate partner.
- 1 in 7 women have been stalked by an intimate partner.
- Domestic violence hotlines in America receive over 20,000 calls daily.
- Domestic violence accounts for 15% of all reported violent crime.

Drug Possession

Criminal drug possession refers to the unlawful control or ownership of controlled substances, as defined by applicable local, state, or federal statutes. It involves knowingly and intentionally having illegal drugs in one's possession, such as narcotics or controlled substances, without proper authorization, prescription, or legal justification.

The Controlled Substances Act categorizes drugs into specific Schedules, according the drug's medicinal use and proneness to abuse.

- Schedule 1: marijuana, heroin, LSD, ecstasy, and magic mushrooms.
- Schedule 2: cocaine, meth, Oxycodone, Adderall, Ritalin, and Vicodin.
- Schedule 3: Tylenol with codeine, ketamine, anabolic steroids, and testosterone.
- Schedule 4: Xanax, Soma, Darvocet, Valium, and Ambien
- Schedule 5: Robitussin AC, Lomotil, Motofen, Lyrica, and Parepectolin.

Many of the brand named drugs listed above are trademarked and patented names. They are listed here to illustrate the type of drugs in each Schedule, as set by the Drug Enforcement Agency. It is not intended as criticism of their medicinal value, when legally prescribed and used.

Interestingly, the DEA maintains marijuana in Schedule 1, right next to heroin and LSD. Additionally, many drugstores now require a customer to show ID to purchase cough medicine, as it is routinely used in the manufacture of meth.

The severity of charges for illegally possessing drugs may vary based on the type and quantity of drugs involved, and their respective Schedule. Complicating this issue is the conflict between state and federal jurisdictions. For example, at the federal level possession or use of marijuana is illegal. However, in many states it is not.

Drug Trafficking/Distribution

Criminal drug trafficking is the illegal and intentional transportation, distribution, or sale of controlled substances, as defined by the Drug

Enforcement Agency, under the Controlled Substances Act. Enforcement of trafficking laws commonly crosses multiple jurisdictions, as well as multiple countries.

Penalties for illegal drug trafficking vary, based on the Schedule of the drug seized, the quantity, and of course, the drug dealer's prior record.

DUI/DWI

Driving Under the Influence and Driving While Intoxicated are basically the same thing. The term varies from state to state, but typically means the driver has been caught driving erratically, leading to a breathalyzer or blood test that determines a person's blood alcohol content exceeds the state allowed level.

This charge is becoming even more complicated when the driver may be under the influence of drugs, as a breathalyzer or field sobriety test may not be able to document or prove intoxication.

The Center for Disease Control estimates over 1 million people are arrested each year in America for DUI or DWI. The National

Highway Traffic Safety Administration states 13,384 people died in 2021 in alcohol impaired driving incidents, which is about one third of all traffic fatalities. Despite stiff penalties and public service announcements regarding driving under the influence, the numbers of DUI cases continue to increase.

Interestingly, texting while driving is considered 6 times more dangerous than driving drunk. Each year, texting while driving causes 1.6 million accidents, resulting in 390,000 injuries. Also, viewing or sending a text takes your eyes off the road for 5 seconds. If you're travelling at 60 miles per hour, you will travel over 440 feet in the time it takes to read a text. No bueno.

Embezzlement

Criminal embezzlement implies the willful or intentional misappropriation of money or valuable goods, which is distinct from the accidental or neglectful management of funds.

Legally speaking, embezzlement is the movement of entrusted funds for the perpetrator's personal gain. Embezzlement involves a breach of the duty to manage or safeguard the assets of another party, leading to an illegal diversion of those assets.

An embezzler may typically incur prison time for his or her crimes, and is almost always court ordered to provide restitution…even if that entails garnishing of wages for the duration of the perpetrator's life.

The world of the embezzler has some interesting statistics. According to the Gitnux Market Data Report for 2024:

- Companies with fewer than 150 employees may average over $289,000 in embezzlement losses.
- 30% of embezzlement losses occur over a 5 year period, indicating the patience and slow leak effect of many embezzlers.
- American businesses experienced over $8.3 billion in losses in 2020 due to embezzlement.
- 12% of embezzlement cases involve an employee with a gambling addiction.
- 50% of embezzlement cases occur within a financial institution.
- Amazingly, 55% of embezzlers are female.

- 87% of the time, an embezzler has no prior history or conviction of fraud.

- Recovery of embezzled funds only occurs 19% of the time.

- The real estate sector sees the highest rate of embezzlement, with perpetrators apparently targeting escrow accounts and misdirecting transaction fees.

- An estimated 33% of business bankruptcies attribute theft to their demise.

Extortion

Criminal extortion, is the intentional and unlawful acquisition of property, services, or some other benefit from another individual or entity through the use of force, threats, or intimidation.

Extortionists compel a person to act against his or her will by instilling fear of harm, injury, damage to property, or unfavorable consequences, unless the victim complies with their request.

Extortion differs from bribery where a person is given money or valuable services or goods in exchange for a desired action. Examples include enticing a police officer to ignore illegal acts, or paying a judge to offer a favorable ruling, despite evidence to the contrary. In extortion, the threat of undesirable consequences are used as leverage against a person. For example, threatening to harm a police officer's family if he attempts to arrest a criminal, or threats against a judge's reputation or personal safety if she does not render a favorable ruling for the extortionist.

In an excellent story by Arthur Conan Doyle called *The Master Blackmailer*, Sherlock Holmes investigates a man who uses secretive and revealing letters to extort his victims.

Technically, the master blackmailer is an extortionist, not a blackmailer. However, he does use bribery to pay maids and personal servants to collect dirt on his victims. He then uses extortion to threaten to destroy the reputations of his victims unless they pay him.

Forgery

Forgery is commonly thought of as using a fake signature on a document to secure financial gain, such as signing a business partner's name on a document to obtain a business loan.

But forgery goes well beyond fake signatures. Forgery also includes the creation of fake documents, such as checks, property deeds, and art work. The key to a criminal charge of forgery is in the "intentional" act of creating a forgery for financial gain.

The two key elements of criminal forgery:

- Fraudulent intent.
- The creation and use of the forged document.

According to FBI crime data for 2022:

- 23% of offenders in the counterfeiting and forgery category were age 30-39, and 21% were age 20-29.
- 18% of victims of counterfeiting and forgery were age 60-69, and 16% were age 50-59.
- The location of counterfeiting and forgery occurred in banks 23% of the time, and in homes 16% of the time.
- In 28% of the cases involving counterfeiting or forgery, 28% of the time, the victim and offender did not know each other, and in 6% of the cases, the offender and victim were friends.

Fraud

Criminal fraud is a deliberate and deceptive act that uses false representation, concealment of facts, and misleading claims to induce another party to make decisions or take action to their own detriment.

Fraud includes:

- Wire fraud.
- Securities fraud.
- Mail fraud.

The FTC received 2.8 million complaints of fraud in 2021, for a total loss of $5.8 billion.

Harassment

Criminal harassment is intentional and repetitive conduct designed to intimidate, create fear, or cause distress to another.

Typical examples of harassment involve cyber bullying, stalking, and physical proximity. Punishment for harassment generally starts with a restraining order. Violation of this restraining order can lead to fines and imprisonment.

- In the United States, approximately 1.5 million restraining orders are issued annually.
- 70% of all restraining orders are issued to protect women.
- The vast majority of restraining orders are issued to protect people between the age of 18-34.
- 85% of all restraining orders are related to domestic violence.
- Restraining orders reportedly reduce the rate of physical violence against the requester by 80%.
- 30% of individuals named in restraining orders violate the terms of the order.

Hate Crimes

Charges of committing a hate crime are generally used as enhancements to other crimes, such as assault, battery, and property damage. Legally, a hate crime is a criminal offense against another person based on bias or prejudice.

For example, physically attacking or threatening a person based on his or her race, religion, ethnicity, sexual orientation, gender identity, or disability, may lead to a hate crime charge.

According to the FBI, there were 11,634 cases of hate crimes in America in 2022. The majority of these offenses were motivated by hate, bias, or prejudice in five categories:

- Race 59.1%
- Religion 17.3%
- Sexual Orientation 17.2%
- Gender Identity 4%
- Disability 1.5%

66.1% of all hate crime cases in 2022 occurred against persons, and 31.8% of cases involved crimes against property.

Homicide

Homicide is the unlawful killing of a human, and includes varying degrees of culpability, such as first and second degree. Notably, the word homicide is a generic term that includes murder, manslaughter, and justifiable homicide. Murder is the intentional killing of another person, while manslaughter is the accidental killing of a person. Justifiable homicide occurs when a person kills in self defense, or when a police officer lawfully takes a life in the line of duty. 1,144 persons were shot and killed by police officers in 2023.

- 31% of homicide offenders are age 20-29.
- 19% of homicide offenders are age 30-39
- Surprisingly, the age group 10-19 accounts for 18% of homicides.
- 28% of homicide victims are age 20-29.
- 24% of homicide victims are age 30-39.
- 14% of homicide victims are age 40-49.
- Firearms were the weapon of choice in homicide cases 67% of the time.
- 8% of homicides used a knife.
- 45% of homicides occurred in a home.
- 28% of homicides occurred on a highway, street, or sidewalk.
- 7% of homicides occurred in a parking garage or parking lot.
- 12% of homicide victims knew their attacker.
- 9% of homicide victims did not know their attacker.

- 7% of homicide victims were in a relationship with their attacker.

Homicide related statistics and percentages rarely add up to 100% due to a 48% unsolved homicide rate in America today.

Identity Theft

Criminal identity theft is the fraudulent acquisition and use of another individual's personal information, such as name, birth date, Social Security number, and banking details. Sadly, much of the information an identity thief needs to steal another person's identity is available in discarded mail, easily accessible government birth certificates, and victim responses to "data mining" operations disguised as survey and opinion polls.

Identity thieves typically use their ill-gotten information to open bank accounts, establish lines of credit, and apply for Social Security and/or welfare benefits with the intent to essentially rob their victims of money, pensions, and government benefits.

According to Consumer Affairs:

- Identity theft has risen by over 584% over the past 20 years.

- The 30-39 age group accounts for 26% of all reported identity theft cases in 2022.

- Credit card fraud was the most common type of reported identity theft in 2022, with over 441,000 cases.

Insurance Fraud

Insurance fraud is the deliberate and deceptive act of providing false information or engaging in intentional acts to obtain illegitimate insurance benefits.

Insurance fraud includes schemes like submitting false claims, staging accidents, or exaggerating losses to extract financial compensation from insurance companies. Insurance fraud con artists abuse the system for personal gain, causing financial harm to insurers and policyholders.

- Insurance is big business. In America, there are 7,000 insurance companies that collect over $1 trillion in annual premiums.

- The FBI estimates the total cost of insurance fraud at $40 billion per year.

- American consumers see premium increases of $400 and up annually due to fraud.

Interestingly, the most common type of insurance fraud, according to the FBI, is a scam known as "Premium Diversion."

Premium Diversion is when an insurance agent or independent agency, collects premiums from its customers, but pockets the premium, rather than provide it to the underwriter. When the customer requires assistance from his or her insurance, such as in an automobile accident, he or she discovers the coverage has lapsed due to nonpayment of premiums.

Kidnapping

Kidnapping is the criminal act of unlawfully and intentionally seizing, abducting, confining, or restraining an individual against his or her will, with the intent to help in the the commission of a felony, extract a ransom, inflict bodily harm, or interfere with the victim's liberty.

Kidnapping involves the deprivation of personal freedom through force, threat, or deception, resulting in the victim being held captive or detained, typically to collect a ransom for the victim's safe return, or to coerce another person or company to act in a way deemed advantageous to the kidnappers.

- FBI and other crime watch agencies estimate less than 350 kidnappings per year are stranger abductions.
- Kidnapping a person who is 17 or younger is deemed a child abduction.
- Child Find of America estimates up to 2,300 children are missing in America on any given day. That does not mean 2,300 children are added to the missing children roles daily. It means the running average of active missing children cases. This figure includes abductions and runaways.

Regarding abductions, the Child Find of America organizations statistics indicate:

- 78% of abductions involve a non-custodial parent
- 6-11 year old children make up 35% of all abduction cases.
- 24% of abductions are resolved in less than a month.

- 42% of abducted children were living with a single parent.
- 66% of abducted children were taken by a male relative.

On a side note, one of the funniest stories ever written about kidnapping is *The Ransom of Red Chief*, by O. Henry. The O. Henry story was adapted in the movie remake of *Dennis the Menace* with Walter Matthau when Dennis is kidnapped by a hobo.

Larceny

Larceny is the unlawful taking and removal of another person's property with the intent to permanently deprive them of it. Petty larceny typically involves the theft of items of lower value, often classified as misdemeanors, and is subject to less severe penalties. Grand larceny, on the other hand, pertains to the theft of higher-value items and is considered a felony, carrying more substantial legal consequences.

Every state varies, but a threshold of $750 to $1,000 is a typical dividing line between petty and grand larceny. Petty theft usually nets fines, probation, and community service punishments, however, the felony levels of grand larceny may land a thief in prison.

The distinction between larceny and burglary is that burglary involves breaking and entering. For example, if a person is walking down the street and see a bicycle leaning against a telephone pole, stealing the bike with zero intent of returning it, constitutes larceny. However, if the thief unlawfully enters the bicycle owner's garage and steals the bike, the thief has committed burglary.

Manslaughter: Involuntary

Involuntary manslaughter is the killing of another person through negligence. There is no premeditation, and no intent to kill.

For example, if a baseball player loses his temper and throws a baseball bat towards the dugout in anger, and the bat sails into the bleachers and hits a man eating a red hot, causing him to choke on his $8 hot dog, that is involuntary manslaughter. The batter had no intention of harming the fan, and certainly had nothing to do with the fan ordering an over priced hot dog.

A situation like this would be deemed a tragic accident. However, since the batter threw the bat in a reckless or negligent manner, he may be charged with involuntary manslaughter.

The most common use of the involuntary manslaughter charge involves drunk driving. When a drunk driver crashes into another vehicle, or hits a pedestrian, he did not intentionally kill a person. But, by driving under the influence, he is guilty of reckless or negligent homicide.

Manslaughter: Voluntary

Voluntary manslaughter suggests the killer intentionally inflicted harm upon his or her victim. The key to being charged with manslaughter and not murder is the killer's state of mind. Typically, persons guilty of voluntary manslaughter acted in the heat of passion, with no premeditation.

For example, if a man arrives home from work early and finds the mailman in bed with his wife, and in an explosive burst of anger throws the mailman out the window, in reckless disregard for the mailman's life or safety, he is guilty of manslaughter, not murder.

Money Laundering

Money laundering is a process of disguising the source of money, typically from an illegal act. For example, if a meth distributor rakes in 50 grand per week, he can't just walk into the bank and deposit his illegally obtained cash. Instead, he uses a process of integrating the money into the economy in such a way as to hide its true source.

In the TV series, *Breaking Bad*, Walter White and his wife purchase a car wash that allows cash transactions. By faking transactions at the car wash, they were able to integrate illegally obtained funds into their legitimate business.

Mobs, drug dealers, and other cash flush operators routinely operate legitimate cash businesses as "fronts" to launder their money.

Murder: First-degree

First-degree murder is the most serious form of criminal homicide, involving the intentional killing of another person with premeditation and malice aforethought. Premeditation is the planning and deliberate process of carrying out a murder, while malice aforethought denotes a deliberate disregard for human life.

The FBI grades murder rates in terms of incidences per 100,000 people. Here are the five states or districts with the highest per capita murder rates:

- Washington, D.C. 29.3
- Louisiana 16.1
- New Mexico 12
- South Carolina 11.2
- Alabama 10.9

And the five states with the lowest rates:

- Rhode Island 1.5
- Iowa 1.7
- New Hampshire 1.8
- Utah 2
- Hawaii 2.1

Murder: Second-degree

Second-degree murder differs from First Degree Murder in that the killer did not premeditate the murder. However, he or she did have malice aforethought, that is, they knew their actions would cause serious bodily harm, including death.

N.A.P.

A NAP is not a criminal. He or she is a victim. It is included here to reveal how some victims may be considered or treated by law enforcement.

The NAP acronym stands for: Not A Person. It is a demeaning way to describe a crime victim as not important, or not even a "real" person. This derogatory descriptor is sometimes used to describe crime victims who may be drug addicts, prostitutes, or homeless persons. The term is rarely used in official reports, but may be heard in casual conversations between detectives and police officers discussing a case.

Obstruction of Justice

Obstruction of justice is the intentional disruption of a legal proceeding. It may take the form of unruly behavior or protesting in a courtroom, lying to investigators, interfering with a jury, intimidating witnesses, or even withholding or destroying information relevant to a case from the court.

Open Container

An open container, in legal terms, is any receptacle holding alcoholic beverages that has a broken seal, been partially consumed, or lacks its original seal and is readily capable of being consumed.

The intention behind having an open container law is to prevent the drinking of alcoholic beverages while driving.

Parole Violation

Parole is built on trust. The court agrees to the early release of a prisoner, provided he or she promises not to return to life of crime. A paroled convict is "violated" when he or she is observed committing a crime, or in some manner violating the terms of the court agreement that led to his or her early release from prison.

The most common form of punishment for a parole violation is for the convict to be re-incarcerated to finish serving his or her original prison sentence.

Perjury

Perjury is the willful act of intentionally providing false or misleading information while under oath during legal proceedings, such as testimony in court, affidavits, or depositions. There are two keys to a perjury charge. First, the false statements must be relevant to the case, and second, the person making the false statements must be aware his or her statements are false or misleading.

Ponzi Schemes

A Ponzi scheme is a fraudulent investment strategy that promises high returns with little or no risk to investors. The operation relies on using funds from new investors to pay returns to earlier investors, creating an illusion of profit.

Ponzi Schemes typically collapse when the operator can no longer attract new investments or meet the promised returns, leading to widespread financial losses. Ponzi Schemes are named after investment advisor, Charles Ponzi, who popularized the tactic in the early 20th century. Over several years, Ponzi defrauded his clients of over $15 million. Since then con artists have used his techniques to defraud consumers of billions.

One of the most notorious Ponzi Schemes was carried out by an investor and financial advisor name Bernard "Bernie" Madoff. Madoff was convicted of several miscarriages of justice and sentenced to 150 years in prison and court ordered to forfeit $170.9 billion dollars in June of 2009.

Probation Violation

Probation violation occurs when an individual, placed on probation as an alternative to incarceration, fails to adhere to the court-ordered conditions. These conditions may include regular check-ins, avoiding criminal activities, or completing community service.

Once a violation is established, consequences may include warnings, modified conditions, or revocation of probation. The latter could lead to imprisonment, reinstatement of the original sentence, or additional penalties.

According to Bureau of Justice Statistics relevant to probation and parole:

- Approximately 3,745,000 individuals in America are on probation or parole at any given time.
- 1 in 69 American residents were under some form of community supervision at the end of 2021.
- Using the FBI's popular per capita format for crime statistics, 1,143 per 100,000 adult U.S. residents were on probation at the end of 2021.

Prostitution

Prostitution, known as the world's oldest profession, is the exchange of sexual services for financial or material gain. Typically considered a criminal offense, its legality varies globally and within jurisdictions. Participants involved may include sex workers, clients

(Johns), and intermediaries (Pimps). Laws often criminalize aspects such as solicitation, pimping, or operating brothels to curb associated issues like human trafficking and public nuisances.

The word "hooker" is often used to describe a person engaged in prostitution. The origin of the slang term is believed to have come from two sources. First, prior to the American Civil War a New York City neighborhood known as Corlear's Hook was infamous for its brothels and a favorite stopping point for sailors.

The second source of the term comes from the American Civil War and a Union General named Joseph Hooker.

General Joseph Hooker was a notoriously raucous man who loved to host wild parties. According to General Fighting Joe Hooker, "I ain't here for a long time, I'm here for a good time."

Women who followed General Hooker's unit into battle, presumably to keep the troops entertained, came to be known as Hookers.

- Prostitution is dangerous. 204 out of every 100,000 prostitutes die on the job, nearly twice the rate of an Alaska fisherman.

- Between 70,000 and 80,000 people are arrested for prostitution annually in America.

- 70% of prostitution arrests are female, 20% male, and 10% clients.

A common misconception is the legality of prostitution in Las Vegas. It is not. Prostitution is legal in 10 counties within the state of Nevada; however, it is not legal withing the city limits of Las Vegas.

Psychopath

Being a psychopath is not in itself a crime. Its definition is included here to clarify how it differs from sociopaths.

Psychopaths are typically fearless, they enjoy taking risks, they can be charming, and are very methodical and persistent. From this you may think…what's the big deal? They sound like any courageous entrepreneur or successful person. However, there is a darker side.

Psychopaths:

- Lack empathy for others.

- Have low impulse control.

- Feel no remorse.

- Enjoy causing pain in others (sadistic).

- Are pathological liars.

Public Intoxication

Public intoxication is the act of being visibly drunk or under the influence of substances to the extent that one poses a danger to oneself or others in a public place.

The enforcement of public intoxication rules comes down to a police officer's intent to maintain public order and safety.

Racketeering/RICO

Racketeering, under the Racketeer Influenced and Corrupt Organizations Act (RICO), is a federal statute targeting organized criminal enterprises, such as cartels, mobs, and even political organizations.

RICO defines racketeering activity as a pattern of two or more related criminal acts within ten years, including offenses such as fraud, bribery, money laundering, and extortion. The primary power behind RICO prosecution is the ability to charge individuals for the actions attributed to the organization, while not being able to pin those acts on specific individuals. In essence, you can be charged for guilt by association under RICO.

Rape

Rape is a despicable crime against another human being that involves the forceful and non-consensual act of sexual intercourse. Rapists typically use physical violence, threats, incapacitation, and coercion against their victims.

The core aspect of rape is the lack of consent. Consent must be freely given, informed, and enthusiastic. Deviation from this basic principle of consent constitutes rape and can lead to serious criminal charges against the perpetrator.

Even when consent is given, a person may still be charged with rape if the victim is developmentally disabled and deemed by the state to not be capable of giving consent. Also, sexual relations with a minor may constitute statutory rape, as the victim is not old enough to offer consent.

According to national statistics:

- 20% of all women in the United States have been raped in their lifetime.
- 1 in 71 men have been raped in their lifetime.
- 46.7% victims of rape in the United States were raped by an acquaintance.

Robbery

Robbery is a criminal offense involving the use of force, intimidation, or threat to unlawfully take another person's property or belongings while in their presence.

Distinguished from theft by the element of violence or the fear of harm, robbery directly endangers the victim. The intent is to deprive the individual of his or her possessions against their will, by creating a sense of immediate danger.

Armed robbery implies the robber is armed with a lethal weapon, which typically infers a firearm, knife, or other menacing weapon. Strong armed robbery differs slightly from armed robbery, where the criminal is not armed, but threatens to cause harm to his or her victims if they do not comply.

Securities Fraud

Securities fraud encompasses deceptive practices in the financial markets involving the manipulation, misrepresentation, or concealment of information related to securities transactions.

Perpetrators of securities fraud typically engage in insider trading, false statements, or other fraudulent activities to gain an unfair advantage or deceive investors, including "pump and dump" schemes where the con artists talk up a stock just before selling it.

The Securities Exchange Act imposes criminal and civil liabilities, including fines and imprisonment for securities fraud.

Sexual Assault

Sexual assault is a criminal act involving non-consensual sexual contact or behavior imposed on an individual through force, coercion, or incapacitation.

It encompasses a range of offenses, from unwanted touching to rape, in violation of the victim's consent.

Legally defined, consent must be freely given, informed, and voluntary. Protected classes like minors and developmentally disabled persons are not deemed able to offer informed consent.

Shoplifting

Shoplifting is a criminal offense where a thief removes property from a retail establishment without paying for it.

Shoplifting includes actions such as concealing items, altering price tags, switching packaging to avoid detection, and creative checkout practices in self checkout registers.

Current trends in retail shoplifting also include flash mob raids on stores, where a large group of people descend on a store location at the same time and fill shopping carts and backpacks with merchandise, with the intention or reselling the merchandise. Sadly, this practice has led to the closure of dozens of retail establishments, as well as the growing practice of retail stores securing items prone to theft behind locked cabinets.

Laws addressing shoplifting vary by jurisdiction, including some controversial laws in places like California and Illinois that limit charges for shoplifting to cases where the value of the theft exceeds a certain amount, such as $950 in California.

Sociopath

Being a sociopath is not in itself a crime. Its definition is included here to clarify how it differs from psychopaths.

Sadly, we may all harbor some of the key traits of a typical sociopath. Beyond a penchant for rebelling or breaking the law, a sociopath:

- Can be physically aggressive.

- Loves to manipulate others for personal gain.

- Has unpredictable mood swings.

- Tends to have impulsive behaviors.

- Is notoriously unreliable in relationships.

Solicitation

Solicitation is a criminal act involving the intentional request, inducement, or encouragement of another person to engage in unlawful activities, often with the aim of committing a crime.

Solicitation is often associated with prostitution, but may also include inducement to purchase or use illegal drugs, as well as a host of other crimes.

Stalking

Stalking is a criminal behavior characterized by a pattern of repeated, unwanted attention, harassment, contact, or any other behavior directed towards a specific person, causing fear or emotional distress.

It often involves persistent and intrusive actions such as following, monitoring, or communication against the victim's will. Laws addressing stalking aim to protect individuals from the serious emotional and physical harm it can inflict.

Tax Evasion/Fraud

Tax evasion, also known as tax fraud, is the deliberate act of deceiving tax authorities to avoid paying owed taxes. It involves willful misrepresentation or manipulation of financial information, such as under reporting income, inflating deductions, or hiding assets in offshore bank accounts and investments.

The infamous Chicago mafia boss, Al Capone, was convicted and imprisoned on charges of tax evasion.

Telemarketing Fraud

Telemarketing fraud refers to deceptive practices conducted via telephone to unlawfully obtain money or sensitive information from individuals.

Telemarketing scam artists often use false representations, such as fake business opportunities or charities, to exploit victims. Common schemes include prize promotions, fake investments, or deceptive sales tactics.

Theft

Theft is the unlawful taking of another person's property with the intent to permanently deprive them of it.

This act encompasses various forms, such as larceny, shoplifting, embezzlement, and burglary.

Vandalism

Vandalism is a criminal act involving the intentional destruction, defacement, or damage to another person's property without their consent.

This offense encompasses various forms, such as graffiti, property destruction, or tampering with public or private structures.

White Collar Crimes

White-collar crimes are non-violent, financially motivated offenses committed by individuals, businesses, or government professionals in positions of trust and authority. These crimes typically involve deceit, concealment, or violation of trust and are characterized by sophistication and a focus on financial gain.

Examples include fraud, embezzlement, insider trading, and money laundering.

Wire Fraud

Wire fraud is a criminal offense involving the use of electronic communication, such as phone calls or emails, to deceive others for financial gain.

Perpetrators engage in fraudulent schemes, misrepresenting information, making false promises, or manipulating victims into transferring money electronically. Phishing scams using spam emails is an example of wire fraud. Also, most telemarketing scams become cases of wire fraud when the victim is coerced into revealing banking information.

www.ingramcontent.com/pod-product-compliance
Lightning Source LLC
Chambersburg PA
CBHW081515250726
48659CB00009B/2820